Emoti-coms

DATE DUE

Demco, Inc. 38-293

About the Authors

Xavier Quattrocchi-Oubradous is an artist-turned-investment-banker-turned-media-entrepreneur. After many years of cello practice, trying unsuccessfully to emulate his family roots, he graduated in management at Dauphine University, Paris and in political sciences at Sciences Po, Paris. His business career started with financing industrial projects at investment banks Calyon and GE Capital. He then launched a series of businesses in the marketing and communications industry – including QobliQ, a multinational group offering digital, sponsorship, corporate social responsibility (CSR), social media and experiential marketing services. He has published several articles in *Admap*.

Dr Charles Bal was research manager and is now head of brandRapport France, a sponsorship and associative marketing consultancy owned by QobliQ Group. He has developed a new family of sponsorship measurements that take into account the highly emotional nature of sponsorship. As part of a *cotutelle* agreement between the University of Paris-1 Panthéon Sorbonne (France) and the University of Adelaide (Australia), in 2010 Charles completed a PhD examining the role played by emotions in the sponsorship persuasion process. He has already presented his results at marketing conferences in Europe and Asia-Pacific, and has published his work in several international reviews (*Journal of Sponsorship*, *Asia-Pacific Journal of Marketing & Logistics*, *Admap*).

Emoti-coms

A MARKETING GUIDE TO COMMUNICATING THROUGH EMOTIONS

From shouting to singing your message

BY
XAVIER QUATTROCCHI-OUBRADOUS
& CHARLES BAL

Hh

HARRIMAN HOUSE LTD

3A Penns Road
Petersfield
Hampshire
GU32 2EW
GREAT BRITAIN

Tel: +44 (0)1730 233870
Fax: +44 (0)1730 233880
Email: enquiries@harriman-house.com
Website: www.harriman-house.com

First published in Great Britain in 2011

Copyright © Harriman House Ltd

The right of Xavier Quattrocchi-Oubradous and Charles Bal to be identified as
the Authors has been asserted in accordance with the Copyright, Design and
Patents Act 1988.

ISBN: 978-1-906659-72-1

British Library Cataloguing in Publication Data
A CIP catalogue record for this book can be obtained from the British Library.

Cover design by Sophie Blair (www.sophieblair.com).

Set in Caslon, Ubuntu Titling and Ubuntu.

Printed and bound in the UK by CPI Antony Rowe, Chippenham
and Eastbourne

Hh Harriman House

A mes filles, reines de la communication émotionnelle.
– XQO

To my emotions…and to those of you who trigger them!
– Dr Charles Bal

Contents

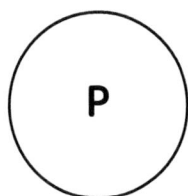 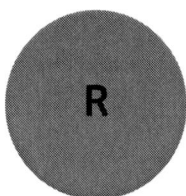 

 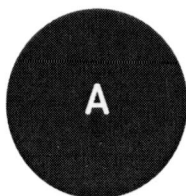 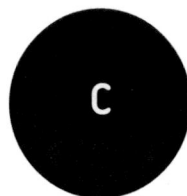

" Music is the shorthand of emotion. "

– Leo N. Tolstoy

A Note on Emotional Communication

T his book makes a number of cross-references to music, which may seem strange as we are dealing with business, marketing and communication.

The first reason for these references is that it is somewhat difficult to talk about emotions in the abstract. Our vocabulary is inadequate for explaining what happens when emotional messages reach our brains, and how we react to these stimuli, as the emotional phenomenon is extremely complex and sometimes counterintuitive. When words are missing, it is often useful to use benchmarks, and the authors' choice has been music.

Why did we choose music?

Like emotions, music has the feeling of a wordless language, almost as complex as spoken or written languages, but communicating with us *directly*, without filter or barrier, and without the necessary treatment of words and syntax. Music does have a grammar, but you do not need to know it in order to listen to it or be deeply affected by it. As Victor Hugo said, "music expresses that which cannot be put into words and cannot remain silent".

That is the reason why the effect of Bach's toccata in D minor is almost immediate on most of us – provoking a flow of thoughts, questions, images; changing our mood, displacing our thoughts, bringing forth a range of new feelings. The first three notes of the toccata, coming out of the organ's pipes, are designed to grab our attention in an instant, divert all of our brain functions towards our ears (or rather towards the vibrations coming through our ears), focus and be ready for the later developments. They are comparable to the first three notes of Beethoven's fifth symphony in the energy, power and excitement they convey. The muezzin's *adhan* (call to prayer) is equally striking. It is difficult to imagine faster ways to generate emotions, apart from fight-or-flight situations.

This is typically what our business readers need to do every day, all day long: grab the attention of their audience to convey a message. This is what music does. And it is what emotionally focused marketing will help us to do more effectively than ever before.

Why music is more relevant than vision in our argument

Visual creations were of course also designed for the purpose of promoting faith or other messages. The Mayan or Egyptian pyramids, Greek or Khmer temples, the Taj Mahal, the Blue Mosque, or even the sorcerer's body paintings and other outlandish attributes are designed to help people apprehend some sense of the divine – by showing them something at the limits of what their brain can believe, something almost unfathomable.

WHY DO WE LOVE TO BE DECEIVED?

What is the common factor between a bestselling novel, a great movie, a hilarious joke, a jaw-dropping presentation and an illusion? For American cognitive neuroscientist Al Seckel, the common denominator is simple.

They all violate our expectations in some sort of pleasing way.

Human beings have a natural tendency to anticipate what is going to happen, and to form expectations about their near future. In some cases, a violation of their expectations is perceived negatively because of disruptions it brings to their life. But on the other hand, when the situation is not critical and the trick is clever, an unexpected twist can be a joyful experience.

This is precisely what happens when we are exposed to an illusion. Irrespective of our age, social background or experiences, there is always something fascinating in being confronted with a visual representation that literally tricks our brains; an image, for instance, that fools the most primal of our senses, making us see a circle when it is actually a square, or a moving 3D shape when the reality is a fixed 2D drawing.

What Al Seckel's work teaches us is that not only are we easily fooled, but we somehow like it. Our brains usually 'produce' positive emotions when we partake of these illusions. We enjoy being willingly deceived.

However, the main difference between visual messages and music, and the reason why music is a more helpful analogy for discussing emotions, is that it too deals with less direct, objective, measurable experiences. We have difficulty in explaining why we are touched by sonorous harmonies – but we can easily describe how impressed we are by the height of a cathedral in comparison to our human body size, or the pleasing colourful effect of sunlight through stained glass. Our brains can deconstruct, rationalise and explain the complexity of the visual message – especially as the brain capacity in processing visual messages is highly developed.

Conversely, harmonic sounds and rhythm resonate directly with the brain, since the equivalent of the treatment of eye-sourced information by the visual cortex is almost nonexistent in hearing.[1] Music has a more direct and straightforward impact on our brains. This means the musical effect is much closer to the influence of emotions in the brain than vision.

Why music is more relevant than odours

Deeply nested in our evolutionary roots, thus wired even more deeply and more directly than hearing and sight into our brain, smell is probably the only other sense that is a reasonably close parallel for the operation of emotions. Like emotions, smells are instantly and effortlessly provocative. A famous example is given by French novelist Marcel Proust, who described how the simple act of smelling his mother's cake brought back a veritable flood of memories.

However, there is no form of smell-based emotional creation, apart from food and drink, that can strictly be considered a form of art, a method of communication. Smell is more related to pure survival – detecting enemies and inedible food in the infancy of mankind as a species – and this is why there is no art related to that sense. In the context of marketing and communication, smell is almost impossible to use as a channel or raw material, despite some unsuccessful past attempts, and the classic of the artificial – and so delicious – croissant smell pumped out from some bakeries. This is why it would have been difficult to use the smell sense to explain how important emotions convey messages to audiences.

Music-related brain circuitry is of business interest

Music at Mass or other religious gatherings can be compared to background music in shops, aimed at creating a sense of wellbeing for the public and enabling higher buy-out levels. Environmental psychologists Mehrabian and Russell's (1974) research shows that individuals respond emotionally to background music, which creates an "approach-avoidance" behaviour favourable to mental or financial buy-out; a technique used in bars, restaurants and retail shops to increase consumption.

A series of studies run by North, Hargreaves and McKendrick (1997, 1998 and 1999) have shown how important music can be for business. For instance, they demonstrated that music could influence customers' perception of a store or a bar; that in-store music could prolong customers' visits and increase staff productivity. In a very interesting experiment (see the boxout 'Listening is drinking'), they even showed that music could directly influence customer choice.

LISTENING IS DRINKING

In 1999 research was undertaken to investigate whether stereotypical French and German music could influence the selection of French and German wines. Over a two-week period, French and German music was played on alternate days at an in-store display of evenly priced wines.

Results show that French music led to French wines outselling German wines 3:1 and the German music led to the German wines outselling the French wines 2:1. And when customers were questioned leaving the store, they were unaware of any effects and denied having been influenced by any music!

Source: North A.C., Hargreaves D.J., and McKendrick J. (1999). 'The influence of in-store music on wine selections', *Journal of Applied Psychology*, 84, 271-276.

All this, we feel, justifies our choice of music as a benchmark for the difficult exercise of explaining how emotions reach our brains.

The techniques used by any marketing communicator will try to emulate how powerful music is in penetrating something deep into the audience's brain – not to say 'heart', being a deeper part of the brain – which is ultimately where a message should reach.

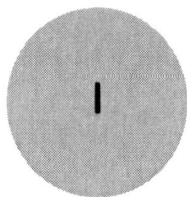 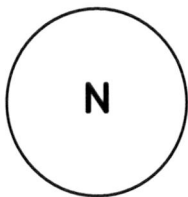 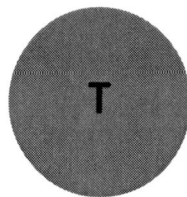

 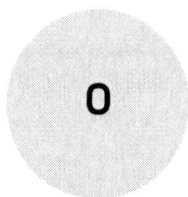 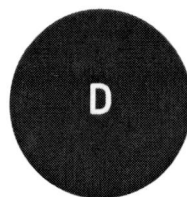

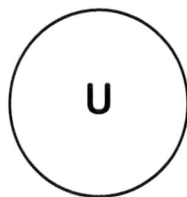  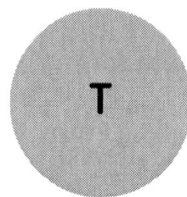

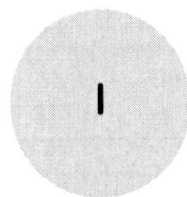 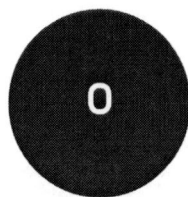 

" " Here is my secret. It is very simple: It is only with the heart that one can see rightly; what is essential is invisible to the eye. " "

– Antoine de Saint-Exupéry

Reversing the Eyeball-to-Eyewall Trend

A famous if controversial study from American psychologist Albert Mehrabian, published in 1967, concluded on the supremacy of non-verbal communication cues over verbal and vocal ones.[2]

According to him, spoken words, voice tone and facial expressions respectively contribute 7%, 38% and 55% to the understanding of someone's communication. Put differently, words alone often lack the substance and the subtlety that enable the understanding of a spoken message.

This is why most of us needing to seriously engage another person, for business or personal purposes, would do so (in decreasing preference) by:

1. meeting in person

2. video conference

3. phone call

4. email, SMS, instant chat, fax or mail

5. and more and more rarely, telegraph or smoke signals.

In this time of mass communications and increasingly powerful communication tools, there is something highly ironic in the fact that most of the understanding of a message is disconnected from what has always typically been thought of as the clearest communication medium: words. Indeed, we experience this daily in both our personal and professional communications with others; the words we use in an email, for instance, cannot ever convey the reassurance of a smiling face. A letter of complaint struggles hard to transmit, with half the efficiency, the opprobrium of one's tone of voice on a phone call to an errant customer services department.

Having this in mind, it is easy to understand why we invest so much time and effort in phrasing and rephrasing our thoughts when words and to a lesser extent, tone, are the only medium we can use (as is the case in emails, phone calls, instant chat…). Funnily enough, one of the most common solutions we have found to overcome this verbal inefficiency is precisely to introduce *emoticons* – nothing more than faces representing expression or tone – into personal and (more and more often) into professional correspondences that take place in this medium.

The central idea we propose in this book is that words or images alone are insufficient most of the time to communicate in a business environment, and, more specifically, when marketing or communicating messages.

> **"The central idea we propose in this book is that words or images alone are insufficient most of the time to communicate in a business environment, and, more specifically, when marketing or communicating messages."**

The power of communication does not reside in the spoken, but rather in the unspoken; not in the seen, but in the 'felt'. In other words, in the *emotional*: in a range of non-spoken cues, widely and consistently understood by each and every one of us. And all communicators – individuals or professionals – have to go beyond the word, and even the image, to reach the emotional part of the brain in order to make sure their message is properly understood and memorised.

There is nothing new in affirming that emotions add richness and depth to communication. That said, traditional and (now ageing) new media still show us every day how stubbornly reliant mainstream communication is on the *power of words or images alone.* The authors believe this is due to a lack of understanding of the phenomenon of emotions, a concern as to their elusiveness, rather than a genuine attempt to privilege 7% (words) over 93% (tone and expression, the emotional dimension). Part of the aim of this book is, simply, to remedy this.

● ○ ○

On the particular topic of sight and visual cues, a study from Bohn and Short (2009) provides us with an amazing – or perhaps terrifying – statistic. Computing 20 different sources of information (newspapers, books, internet, video games, etc), Bohn and Short conclude that the average American consumer is exposed to 100,500 words and 34 gigabytes of visual information flow every day.[3] This means that an average American brain has to deal over its lifetime with close to 1,000 terabytes of data! And again, this only considers visual information.

This is to be compared with what our close ancestors were exposed to: a similar landscape every day, few new faces, no screens or coded language (books, newspapers, web pages), except for those who were literate (fewer and fewer, the further you go back). Probably a couple of gigabytes, not more. So the stretch for our brains has been enormous, especially in the last few decades. We have not found any research on the evolution of this flow over time, but we believe the increase is exponential – and will keep growing; witness, for instance, the current surge in mobile devices: with sales of smart phones and tablets primed, in 2011-2012, to overtake sales of personal computers, giving us access to even more information everyday.[4]

The arguments of this book for a new form of marketing partly depend on the fact that our brains have become wired to avoid the vast bulk of fabricated visual messages. Try, for instance, to write down in exact detail the last web-based advert you saw…Still puzzling over it? Who wouldn't be?

Such aversion to relatively straightforward communication owes much to the emotional dimension of consumption – as we shall see in Chapter 2, any act of consumption is inescapably emotional. And it is not to be wondered that unemotional appeals to plunge us into that affective encounter do not work, especially when ceaseless, unsubtle and uninvited. But it also has another pretty obvious and straightforward explanation: in terms of sheer numbers, it is impossible for the brain to properly compute every promotional message that confronts it; and so it has adapted to block out as many as it can.

"It is impossible for the brain to properly compute every promotional message which confronts it; and so it has adapted to block out as many as it can."

In business terms, this means it is increasingly difficult to convey a message to an audience, whoever they are, through simply showing them a visual or text message. Consumers have built up their perceptual defences just to protect their inner emotional balance, and do not hesitate to engage them. This is what we call the 'eyeball-to-eyewall' effect in this book. We have all learned almost naturally to skip promotional messages that intrude our day-to-day life: 30 second spots in the middle of a TV show, pop-up windows on websites, banners on iPhone or iPad apps – as soon as we feel that someone is trying to illicitly attract our eyeball, our attention immediately turns to something else, our focus changes, we use the remote control, we detach our eyeballs from the screen, we click elsewhere.

In a millisecond we have skipped over it, our brains making sure that the message is not clogging our processing and storage capacity, and cannot start engaging our emotions. The human brain is perhaps uniquely flexible, and adapts its own organisation constantly in order to protect its integrity. This makes the lives of those of us in charge of reaching specific neurons extremely difficult.

Interestingly enough, younger generations – who have always known a high level of promotional noise – are even more efficient at this. They recognise any intrusion and reject it with a speed and severity somewhat wonderful to behold.

On the supply side, there is nothing we can do about this ever-increasing flow of information: our consumption-based economies and lifestyles require the promotion of anything and everything from cars to hairdressers, from pet food to beer, from pension plans to holidays. People do not easily opt-in to promotions of *interest* to them, let alone those which they have not hitherto considered. Brands, products, people, politicians, lobbies and services wanting to reach our brains therefore believe they have to push more and more messages to everyone, statistically reaching their targets but at the same time firing wide more often than not, and contributing to the general bottleneck of communications in our heads.

Despite very low hit rates, the relatively inexpensive process of this broad communication makes it profitable enough to continue and grow. Message owners may try and narrow down their communication to as focused an audience as possible – hence studying their target demographics in detail and using media appropriate to them – but the principle within that niche remains the same. And the consequence for most of us is this overflow of messages, where even the more remote portions of the world are not immune but have their own Coca-Cola billboards and text message spam too.

"This cacophony is going to bother us forever – with our eyewalls mounting ever more quickly – making traditional push-style marketing ever more inefficient."

This eyeball-to-eyewall trend is irreversible given the organisation of our market-driven economies, and will accelerate even further with globalisation – as new products, ideas and services are brought to our decreasing attention.

This cacophony is going to bother us forever – with our eyewalls mounting ever more quickly – making traditional push-style marketing ever more inefficient at the margin: the last of thousands of messages (or gigabit of promotional information) hitting your eyewall in a day has a very slim chance of being considered by your brain.

Innovative solutions are required. This book is meant to be a contribution to that end: a fruitful study of what can be done to stand out amidst the promotional overflow.

The emotional approach

The authors believe that a better way to attract the audience's attention again is not by intensifying the bombardment and hitting the eyewall increasingly harshly in a vain attempt to burst through. It is rather by circumventing it, slipping through it, by leveraging consumers' emotions. *Nothing is more arresting, relevant and memorable to a consumer than what actually affects him or her.*

Indeed, what could be better for a promotional message than to look like any other message of interest (not assault) to the target – such as, say, information related to his or her hobbies, basic instinct needs, feelings? The eyewall would certainly not notice it. To use a musical benchmark, it would be like penetrating the brain as music penetrates the ear (which cannot be stopped), rather than material attempting to penetrate the eye (which can be closed voluntarily).

There is an eyewall, but there is no earwall.

E.g.

LOVE AND HATE AND NIKE

In early 2009, Nike created a viral video – entitled 'Cristiano Ronaldo: Love Him or Hate Him?' – to mark Portuguese football superstar Cristiano Ronaldo's selection as the FIFA Player of the Year. In the 64-second video, supporters of numerous ages and backgrounds hold forth against either 'Love' or 'Hate' signs, sharing what it is about Ronaldo that drives them crazy – in either a good or a bad way.

Nike's video does a great job of tapping into the love/hate relationship that fans have for Ronaldo's way of playing and behaving and how this contributes to who Cristiano Ronaldo is as an athlete and a person.

Interesting in this campaign is the fact that you cannot watch this video without questioning yourself about whether you love or hate Cristiano Ronaldo; in other words, without being engaged at an emotional level, and thereby effectively being folded into participation with the very advert itself (the stars of which are ordinary people just like you).

This is just a very simple, straightforward example of the kind of emotionally engaging marketing that is, we believe, the most effective form for our times – and will be for years to come. The following chapters will show just how and why in clear and, we hope, compelling terms.

- To show what makes emotion the key element in most communications, in the first chapter we discuss the notion of rationality in business and raise its principal limits.

- In the second chapter, we offer a guided tour in the realm of 'affect', furnishing readers with all the appropriate knowledge and insight they need to get on top of a potentially alien area and to start thinking in emotional terms for more effective marketing.

- In the third chapter, we deal with why emotions matter so much to consumers, and begin to look at what is critical in reaching them with longer lasting effect.

- In the fourth, we make things more concrete by presenting a number of communication techniques and examples that use emotions as the main persuasion path.

- Finally, in the fifth chapter, we bring it all together and propose a new communication paradigm, based on a quest for consumers' share of heart (as opposed to the marketers' share of voice and share of market).

  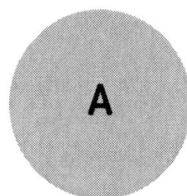

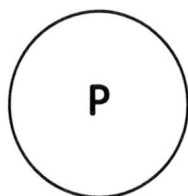 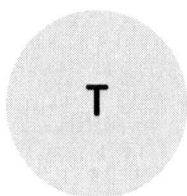 

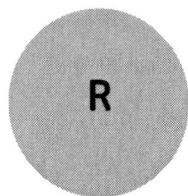 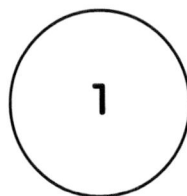

" The reasonable man adapts himself to the world; the unreasonable one persists in trying to adapt the world to himself. Therefore all progress depends on the unreasonable man. "

– George Bernard Shaw

CHAPTER 1

Rationality: A Theory of Economists, a Myth in Business

ationality is a central principle in many scientific
disciplines. It is a philosophical and theoretical
framework that enables explanations of numerous
situations and behaviours in psychology, sociology, economics and
even artificial intelligence. It has also been used to draw the
boundaries of so-called rational thinking and decision-making;
and employed as a synonym for objectivity and cleverness. It has
even been used to discriminate grounded, logic-oriented people
from idle daydreamers.

What is fascinating about rationality in the particular context of
marketing is that it is mostly used to anticipate the behaviours of
an individual – the so-called *rational consumer* – with whom only
few of us can really identify.

Who recognises themselves as an individual focusing only on
the maximisation of the utility of his or her choices (rather than
wellbeing), and employing a computer-like multi-step decision
process for this in every decision of their life? Equally to the point
for marketing, an industry occupied in trying to engage the
aspirations and self-image of consumers, who *wants* to?

And if marketers are accustomed to market testing as a way of anticipating real-world consumer response to their products and marketing, why do they keep using an imaginary rational consumer as a proxy for the normal consumer?

Alfred Hitchcock described what he loved so much about his work with the following words: "drama is life with all the boring bits cut out". In our case, we wished we could have written an entire book talking about emotions "with all the boring bits cut out". But since emotions and emotional behaviour can only be discussed and properly understood when put into the context of cognition and rational behaviour, a chapter dedicated to rationality is a key starting point. One cannot discuss emotionality without talking first about rationality. And we think, in fact, that the implications of this chapter mean that it should prove far from tedious.

1.1 What is rationality?

Etymologically, the word 'rationality' derives from the Latin *ratio* (reckoning, calculating, reasoning), being itself a translation of the ancient Greek *logos* (word, speech, discourse). In its contemporary meaning, the word rationality tends to describe a consistent posture towards the optimal satisfaction of one's goals. The concept of rationality is widely used as a major assumption in most microeconomic models and analysis, but has also become increasingly employed in other social sciences such as sociology and political science.

Generally speaking, rationality theories state that human beings are able to act reasonably, using their discernment to find the solution that suits them the most. This initial assumption has given rise to at least two broad interpretations of how it operates in practice: economic rationality and bounded rationality.

Economic rationality is the utilitarian interpretation of rationality. It says that people compare costs and benefits for all of their decisions in order to maximise their utility. According to this view, the *homo economicus* will consider all of the alternatives, forecast the outcome of each option, weigh up the positives and negatives of each option, balance costs against benefits, and identify the perfect solution, i.e. the one maximising advantages (or gains) and minimising disadvantages (or losses). For the proponents of economic rationality (really starting with Jeremy Bentham and John Stuart Mill), this thought process of selecting a logical choice from among the available options could be applied to explain any decision, in any situation; including the most trivial ones (e.g. buying toothpaste or finding your way in the subway).

This interpretation of rationality has been criticised by many, including Nobel Prize winner Herb Simon (1957), who opposed what he thought of as a dehumanised, computerised view of human beings. He espoused the alternative concept of **bounded rationality**. In this view, individuals' rationality is limited because of their lack of information, their cognitive limitations, and the amount of time they have to make their decisions. His theory leads to the following two adjustments to how to interpret the concept of rationality:

1. **From maximisation to optimisation:** the individual will look for the best solution possible, considering its constraints and limitations.

2. **From optimisation to satisfaction:** aware of their limitations, decision makers will simplify the different options available before applying their rationality. Decision makers are therefore looking for a satisfactory solution rather than the optimal one.

The limited utility of all this utility

Now, in favour of both of these theories, most readers of this book will have been educated and trained to rationalise the world as best they can, especially their economic environment. Everyone is reasonably comfortable with the notions of supply and demand, and cost/benefit analysis. And everyone expects to make the best possible decisions for themselves and for their employees, their business, their stakeholders. Everyday experience and attitudes tell

"What if all this rationality is just a lie we tell ourselves? A very convenient untruth?" us that bounded rationality is probably a far more accurate description of this than the utilitarian efficiency of economic rationality – no man is a machine, after all. But what if even such limited reasoning is putting it too strongly?

What if all this rationality is just a lie we tell ourselves because of the emotional, and not rational, need for a sense of control? And what if it is only accepted by all and sundry, not least marketers, because it is, so to speak, a very convenient untruth?

Applying the concept of rationality to the marketing realm provides marketers with a great prediction pattern. And it makes marketing pleasingly straightforward. When the consumer is rational, someone doing everything they can to spend their money wisely, securing the best deal possible, all the marketer has to do is address themselves rationally to the task of reaching them.

Assuming that consumers will take the most rational action is extremely useful for marketers as it allows a great consistency across the different predictive and analytical models they can use to anticipate and review the effect of promotional campaigns, direct marketing, loyalty programmes, etc.

When studying human behaviours, there is something uncannily expedient in claiming that we all look for the same thing: the optimal situation. Even more convenient for the thinker (be they a psychologist, a sociologist…or a marketer) is the fact that, since everybody is *rational*, they can assume that they will behave according to well-defined behavioural patterns. No complication or unexpected factors impede on their use of predictive models.

But can we really assume that every consumer is obsessed by the optimal satisfaction of his or her personal goals? Or every corporation by the optimal allocation of its resources? Is it reasonable to see the world – especially the marketing world – through a rational lens? Should we sacrifice a realistic representation and understanding of consumption behaviours in the name of convenience? Is it rational to consider people as… rational?

We believe people – consumers and business decision-makers alike – should not be considered rational for a number of reasons, most of which we will look at in a moment. But perhaps the most simple is the most devastating. As we will explain later in this book ('The affective trigger: no decision without emotion' in Chapter 3, page 65), science shows that making a decision is determined by giving your *preference* to a solution, by choosing the option that makes you *feel* the best, the one you are the most *comfortable* with. Affects are simply – we should say, neurologically – essential to making any decision.[5]

"Humans are not designed to make rational decisions."

Reason exists but it is demonstrably guided by emotion. The process can be rational (having an exhaustive view of the different possible solutions, independently assessing the options, and so on), but the decision itself will never be rational.

Humans are not designed to make rational decisions.

1.2 Are we really in control of our decisions?

We have all been confronted by visual illusions at least once in our life. We have all been fooled by illusionists' performances or installations showing something we thought to be moving whilst it was actually static, and fooled again when we were later exposed to the same experience. We have all perceived something *incorrectly* – thus leading to irrational thoughts or behaviours – until the visual trick was revealed and the reality established. And we have all come to ask ourselves: *how is it possible that I didn't see the exact reality at first glance?*

Okay, you might think, but since these are only visual tricks, there is no harm. It is not too much of a big deal to be fooled that easily…Fair enough. But now think about this.

If vision is what we are the best at (brain areas dedicated to vision are bigger than those dedicated to anything else), and if visual illusions prove that we can be predictably and repeatedly wrong, what are the chances that we do not make far more mistakes in something we are not so good at? Something that derives from no dedicated evolutionary development and does not benefit from a dedicated part of the brain?

Something like consumption decisions or the interpretation of marketing communications.

In such matters, the issue might not only be that we make more mistakes, but also that we have greater difficulty in perceiving these mistakes, since it is always harder to demonstrate a cognitive error rather than a visual error (or illusion). The medium of the slip-up (the mind) is the same as the medium where the slip-up must be caught and corrected.

DO WE REALLY KNOW OUR OWN PREFERENCES?

A famous example comes to mind when studying the real rationality of decisions.

In a study by Samuel McClure and his colleagues (2004), 67 people had their brains scanned while being given the 'Pepsi Challenge', a blind taste test of Coca-Cola and Pepsi. Half the subjects chose Pepsi, since the taste of Pepsi happened to produce a stronger response than Coke in their brain's ventromedial prefrontal cortex, a region thought to process feelings of reward.

But when these subjects were told they were drinking Pepsi, three-quarters changed their mind and said that Coke tasted better. Their brain activity had also changed.

The lateral prefrontal cortex, an area of the brain that scientists say governs high-level cognitive powers, and the hippocampus, an area related to memory, were now being used, indicating that the consumers were thinking about Coke and relating it to memories and other impressions and emotionally, rather than rationally, changing their mind.

The results show Pepsi could theoretically – in a rational world – have the same market share as Coke. But in reality, it is split –

with 17% of the soft drink market for Coke versus 9.9% for Pepsi (US, 2009).

We actually do not know our preferences that well. And because we do not really know our preferences, we are vulnerable to the influence of a lot of external forces – even to the point of making ourselves like something more than we objectively do, simply because we think we do.

McClure S.M., Li J., Tomlin D., Cypert K.S., Montague L.M. and Read Montague P. (2004), 'Neural Correlates of Behavioral Preference for Culturally Familiar Drinks', *Neuron*, 44, pp.379–387.

The assumption of rationality is seductive. But it is not a good assumption! It is a misunderstanding of what a human being is, of what a human being's decisions are made of.

The neglect of impulse and involvement

Rationality theories neglect a fundamental pillar of human and consumer behaviours: impulsive acts. Considering that between 70% and 90% of purchase decisions, depending on the type of retail stores, are taken in-store, a model that does not even consider the eventuality of non-premeditated acts cannot be viable.[6] Life itself is a series of decisions, but very rarely are the decisions based on an extensive reviewing of the different possible alternatives, and a 100% logical, cold-blooded choice (as far as pure logic is possible in a consumption situation).

> "We actually do not know our preferences that well. We can be influenced into thinking we like something more than we objectively do."

Furthermore, rationality theories over-simplify what decades of academic research in marketing have demonstrated: the critical importance of *involvement* in the consumer's life. In this context, involvement refers to how much time, thought, energy and other resources people devote to a given purchase process. Generally speaking, the more the consumer is involved, the more rational his decision-making process.

If he has to buy a flat-screen television (high material involvement), a new house (high financial involvement) or a ring for his fiancée (high affective involvement), he will naturally spend more time gathering information and making his decision. This favours the making of a rational decision.

At the opposite end, if he has to buy a toothbrush (low material involvement), a lottery ticket (low financial involvement) or a cinema ticket for his partner (low affective involvement), he will favour a quick decision-making process, requiring few cognitive efforts; a decision-making process that uses what is felt rather than what is thought (and therefore needs to be interpreted). The problem with rationality is that it only provides marketers with the beginning of an understanding of highly involved consumption decisions…and that these kinds of situation simply do not happen every day in a consumer's life.

In addition, as suggested by Shugan (2006), many variables have to be added if one wants to get a realistic picture of actual consumption situations. For example, in the context of a charity auction sale, a consumer might pay a higher price than normal to altruistically raise more money for the charity. Objectively, the decision itself is irrational. It only makes sense when you introduce an affective variable into the equation: here, the positive *feeling* of doing something good.

So what we mean here is that rationality theories offer a too simplistic representation of the consumer world. Rationality theories cannot be used to explain consumer behaviours; they constantly need to be upgraded, with probably as many variables and add-ons as there are consumption situations!

Finally, rationality theories fail to distinguish between a *need* (i.e. something we need in order to survive) and a *want* (i.e. something that is not vital to survive). If the consumer were the rational figure described earlier, his main goal would therefore be to attend to his needs, rather than satisfy his wants. And since truly vital goods and services are rare, if the consumer were really rational, marketing and communication would never be what they are today: trillion dollar industries. Indeed the very industries that marketing serves would scarcely exist. The offerings of every aisle of every supermarket might be reduced to a single box.

Our point is not to say that every action is emotional. Against such a view one could perhaps list parallel objections to those listed against rationality. The reality is that people have always been partly rational, partly emotional. The news is how preeminent the emotional has become.

Recent trends show that consumers are increasingly driven by emotional desires, ranging from pure hedonistic experiences to the quest for 'meaningful consumption': a way of consuming where values and symbols allow the consumer to be at peace with themselves and their decisions, to feel good. This is a thread we shall pick up again in Chapter 3, 'Emotion and consumption: the new pursuit of happiness' (page 62).

1.3 Business is not only about rationality

In a recent TED conference, behavioural economist Dan Ariely said:

> "When it comes to building the physical world, we kind of understand our limitations. [...] And we build around it. But for some reason when it comes to the mental world, when we design things like healthcare and retirement and stock markets, we somehow forget the idea that we are limited."

He is making an important point. When you walk through a city, take the subway or visit the Empire State Building, everything seems rational. The roads are not loop-the-loops, the trains stop before opening their doors, the landmark is not built upside down. Material things are rational because they obey physical, chemical

"The beauty of humanity is the nightmare of marketers."

or biological laws that are simply indisputable. To ignore them is to infallibly be proved a fool.

More seriously, for instance, a heat wave will always dilate the inner structure of a bridge, while an ogive will always require a circular arc of greater radius than the diameter of the cylindrical section to be robust. Attempts to defy this are as sensible and as feasible as trying to walk to the moon.

But when it comes to human matters – to matters of the mind – we are confronted with highly disputable, unwritten, evanescent laws that no one can ever fully master. The beauty of humanity is the nightmare of marketers. Marketing has to build in a world without an equivalent to Newtonian physics, without any sure and certain knowledge of how things must be because of how audiences will respond. When it builds thinking it does so in a rational, predictable universe, it makes the obverse blunder of a designer building a car out of blancmange. It treats its audience like the robots they are not; it misses the greater substance of mankind.

Indeed the characteristics of the so-called 'rational consumer' actually describe another phenomenon in psychology: alexithymia, which means pushing back and ignoring our emotions. Psychologists qualify such a practice as part of a 'personal disorder'.

ALEXITHYMIA – THE EMOTIONAL VACUUM

As terrible as it sounds, certain people are more or less 'emotion proof'. These people are called alexithymics (from the ancient Greek *alexein humos*: pushing back your soul, your emotions) by the psychotherapist Peter Sifneos (1973). They suffer from a form of emotional inhibition that causes difficulty in understanding and describing their emotions; difficulty in differentiating between emotions and bodily expressions of emotions; a low-fantasy imagination, echoing a concrete and reality-based cognitive orientation; and a high degree of social conformity.

Surprisingly, alexithymia is no such thing as an orphan disease, as it affects between 8 and 20% of the world's population, according to different studies. It is not even considered a disease by the psychology community, but a personal disorder.

The irony for marketers is that the emotional vacuum described by alexithymia sounds very similar to the idea of the 'rational consumer' as it is taught in most marketing textbooks. In other words, what psychologists describe as a personal disorder has long been considered the referent pattern by marketers.

In concluding this first chapter, it is interesting to look at two fundamental notions used in psychology:

1. **Theory of mind**, which is the ability – developed during childhood – to understand that other people have their own plans, thoughts and points of view. It therefore also helps us to understand other people's beliefs and intentions. The lack of a 'theory of mind' in a person is usually considered as the main characteristic of autism.

2. **Empathy**, which is the ability to understand and share other people's feelings and emotions. American philosopher Alvin Goldman defined empathy as "the ability to put oneself into the mental shoes of another person to understand her emotions and feelings". In other words, empathy can be seen as the affective – the emotional – counterpart of the theory of mind. A lack of empathy is a lesser characteristic of autism.

The marketing and communications industries are strong on the theory of mind – they know that consumers have a set of intentions and perspectives. But, unlike a psychologically healthy human being, they rarely combine it with empathy and therefore often fail to truly understand or communicate with them.

Why would it be an advantage in business to disregard someone else's emotions or, even worse, your own emotions? How can it be advantageous to keep using rational descriptions of the consumers and rational models (such as exposure equates to visibility, which equates to memorisation, which equates to awareness – the classic axiom of old-school eyeball-attractor marketing) to anticipate their behaviours?

This book offers some solutions to marketers stuck between emotionally driven consumers and executive boards obsessed by measurable returns on investment. It gives them some rationales for demonstrating to their bosses how *irrational* and unrealistic it is to approach the marketing world without an emotional lens. Emotions are obviously not a new variable to consider for marketers; they have always been there. But, as we will see in 2.4, they are gaining more and more importance and space in our societies and simply cannot be ignored or disregarded any more.

This book will also introduce actionable ways of using emotions in communication, and of measuring their effects, furnishing the reader with both the reasons for and the methods of emotionally informed marketing.

We argue in this book that understanding consumers' emotions will allow both the identification of the critical elements that influence their responses to marketing, and the nature of that influence. We will also reveal which communication techniques are the more emotionally charged and which, consequently, are more effective in marketing.

SUMMARY

The irrationality of the rational consumer

- Rational man is both an unrecognisable and neurologically disproved model of a consumer.

- Final choices are always emotional, and consumers are generally only significantly rational in high-end consumption decisions. The decision process might be rational, but the decision itself will always be emotional since it is about giving our preference to one solution rather than another.

- Emotions also lead decisions, even to the point of self-deception in the face of contrary evidence (cf. the test subjects who allowed their emotions to physically make them drop their objective preference for Pepsi in favour of Coke).

- Marketing has hitherto failed to adopt what psychologists would recognise as a healthy mindset towards those very consumers it is meant to be appealing to; it has not yet sought to properly empathise with them.

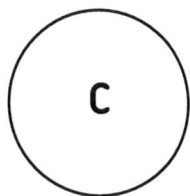 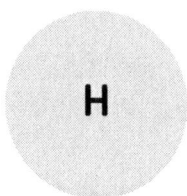 

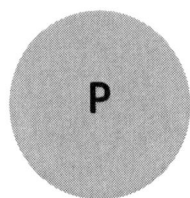  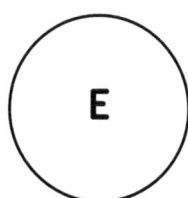

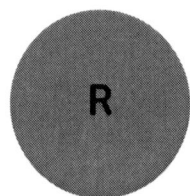 

"There can be no knowledge without emotion. We may be aware of a truth, yet until we have felt its force, it is not ours. To the cognition of the brain must be added the experience of the soul. "

– Arnold Bennett

What We Should Know About Emotions

A s the starting point of a vibrant tribute to Spinoza, the American neurologist Antonio Damasio suggested that none of the objects or people that surround us are emotionally neutral. Everything provokes an emotional reaction, even if only a minimal or an unconscious one. The omnipresence of emotions in interpersonal relationships may be what leads human beings to use them as a major currency when dealing with places, objects and brands.

Nevertheless, despite the central role of emotions in a consumer's day-to-day life, one cannot help but notice that most brands underestimate the power of emotions – when, that is, they are not simply ignoring them altogether.

In our view this lack of consideration is probably due more to marketers' (hitherto) understandably limited actionable knowledge about emotions, rather than a deliberate attempt to banish them from their communications strategies. For this reason, this chapter will offer a series of definitions, key facts and things-to-know about emotions.

2.1 What is emotion?

Standing at the crossroad of several scientific fields, *emotion* is one of those few transversal notions that have captivated almost all branches of science. From philosophy to neurosciences, through sociology, psychology and even biology and theology, each discipline has its own arguments and views about emotions, along with its own definitions of the concept.

Indeed, whichever scientific field you are in, and whatever the subject of your study, taking the emotional dimension into account is rarely ever inappropriate, and frequently produces a bulk of fresh answers and insights – as well as a great deal of new questions.

Thanks to advances in psychology and neurosciences, the boundaries of 'the emotional' are better clarified every day. Knowledge is constantly increasing on the subject of emotion, helping us to better describe what an emotion is, how it operates and how it shapes one's behaviour.

Deconstructing the affective black box

The concept of 'affect' encompasses a wide range of affective reactions, such as emotions, feelings or moods. All these reactions are characterised by the simultaneous occurrence of several things at once: neurophysiological (what happens in your brain during an affect), experiential (what you physically feel during an affect) and expressive (what message you are delivered through the affect).[7]

However, emotions should not be conflated with the distinct (yet related) concepts of mood and feeling. Whilst they all belong to what can be described as the realm of affect, emotion, mood and feeling are different enough to warrant their own definitions.

Moods are long-lasting affective states which cannot be explained by an identified reason nor linked to a particular trigger, but which lead to a range of coherent thoughts and actions. Mood is therefore a general state of mind that is not fully explained or aimed at anything in particular. Consequently, one might consider mood to be the barometer of the relationship one has with one's environment.

This is typically what happens to most of us every so often – when, say, we wake up grumpy, for no apparent reason. The usual behavioural consequences consist of complaining and criticising the entire world, from the weather to the cornering technique of the bus driver. Sometimes until we wake up the next morning!

The musical equivalent of mood is lift music – not excessively painful, nor excessively nice; apparently arbitrary, mostly bothersome.

Feelings are oriented and conscious affective states. According to neuroscientist Raymond Dolan, they are mental representations of physiological changes that characterise someone's affective state.[8] In other words, feelings are nothing more than the conscious experience of an affect. You know what you feel, when and why you feel it and what you will have to do to restore your affective balance.

You 'feel' bad because you said something unfair to a friend of yours. You cannot stop thinking about this conversation and realise that the mere idea of having upset your friend tears you up inside. When your pain becomes unbearable, you apologise to your friend…and start feeling good again.

The musical equivalent of this is when you hear two inharmonious notes, a tuned one and untuned one together (physically: the vibrations not being in phase). You feel uncomfortable; presently deduce the source of the problem; and with the retuning of the problematic note, and the playing of the two notes again (this time in full harmony), the pain subsides and gives way to a sense of relief and balance.

Emotion is a wider and more complex concept than mood or feeling. Describing every side of this phenomenon with any satisfying degree of precision would require an entire collection of books. The simplest way of defining emotions is probably to stick to the basics, and consider them as "a synthesis of subjective experiences, expressive behaviours, and neurochemical activities […] that are part of the human evolutionary legacy and serve adaptive ends".[9]

For instance, the usual emotional reaction to a surprise is also accompanied by a widening of your eyes and a raising of your eyebrows. It is interesting to note that a similar behavioural reaction is also found across other species, like dogs or cats. Such physical reactions are deeply wired into our brains and bodies and come from thousands of years of evolutionary improvements. In this case, it means the range of our senses enlarges in an instant so as to let us evaluate more swiftly whether a surprise we are confronted with is good or bad.

Different emotions provoke different expressive behaviours, of course, and bring with them different neurochemical activities. But they are all part of a blend of physical and psychological reactions and experiences.

A good musical benchmark for this would be for you to close your eyes, picture yourself listening to your favourite piece of music, and analyse what happens deep inside you. After a while you will experience a flow of moods, feelings, thoughts, even physical reactions; you start anticipating the next notes, there is almost a sentiment of fusion between yourself and the music, as if the music's rhythm was organising your thoughts and vital functions, and its harmony carrying you somewhere else. Like an emotion, the music is not simply a mental experience: it goes deeper than that.

Emotions constitute a very disparate collection of behavioural, experiential and social reactions. Some of them can be brief (*embarrassment*) while others can last much longer (*bitterness*); some can be profound (*sadness*) while others are only superficial in nature (*annoyance*); some can have a survival function (*fear*, to escape a danger) others a social function (*disdain*, to express one's disapprobation). Some give way naturally to others; some combine; some reverse. All this leads to the conclusion that emotions should not be considered as a simple and unified collection of mental states, sitting in little mental drawers to be pulled out individually at suitable moments, but rather as a rich and complex family of instinctive psychological states.

In conclusion, emotions strongly influence the way we perceive our environment and genuinely drive our relationships with it. They are a force that helps us react to the thousands and thousands of stimuli that surround us every day, be it promotional, interpersonal or otherwise.

HIERARCHY OF AFFECT

During the past decade, scientists have devoted considerable research attention to the topic of affect. Based on their work, we came to realise that the three different forms of affect we described earlier – moods, feelings, emotions – can be looked at across four comparison-axes, namely *intensity, durability, object-orientation and consciousness.* This allows us to rank, or put into a hierarchy, the different manifestations of the affects. This is shown in the following table.

AFFECT	INTENSITY	DURABILITY	OBJECT-ORIENTATION	CONSCIOUS-NESS
Moods	*	***	*	*
Feelings	**	**	**	***
Emotions	***	**	***	***

Using the musical benchmark can help us to understand the hierarchisation of affect, as shown in the next table.

AFFECT	INTENSITY	DURABILITY	OBJECT-ORIENTATION	CONSCIOUSNESS
MOODS (LIFT MUSIC)	Background sound, not the focus of attention at all.	No beginning or end, can last for days and days.	Perceived as unconstructed music, no theme.	Uninteresting, music is heard but unnoticed.
FEELINGS (PARTY OR CD/RADIO MUSIC)	Listened to (rather than overheard) as part of leisure or relaxation.	Lasts as long as the song; feelings change with the next song.	It is familiar. Humming is a way of easily making the experience more ours.	Can procure a sense of relief; or be really bothersome when repeated too often.
EMOTIONS (CONCERT MUSIC)	Jaw-dropping; mobilising the entire body (goose-bumps).	Has peaks during the performance, but lasts longer than the performance too.	Brings back old memories: the music is a door to experiencing something else.	Captivates the audience, preventing it from doing anything else.

2.2 Six key fundamental facts about emotions

The key finding so far has to be that emotions are **universal**.

1. Emotions are universal

Although each individual does not express them identically, numerous studies show that emotions are experienced similarly across cultures.[10] Emotions are an unspoken language that can be understood by every human being.

Hence, in every country of the world, people will communicate their anger by frowning and their disgust by raising their upper lip. This is a very

> "One consequence is that testing and measuring the result of an emotional stimulus is easier and cheaper for marketers. This can justify a higher investment in planning and executing an emotion-based communication."

interesting fact for anyone wishing to communicate; and very different from purely visual communication like advertising campaigns, which have to be adapted from country to country or from region to region (and even more so from purely verbal communications, which have to be entirely rewritten). One consequence is that testing and measuring the result of an emotional stimulus is easier and cheaper for marketers. This can justify a higher investment in planning and executing an emotion-based communication.The effect of music on individuals is similarly universal. J.S. Bach can be (and is) appreciated across the world, and the fast cultural globalisation of the music industry shows how easy it is to appeal to any listener on the planet.

E.g.

MESSAGE DECLINATION OR UNIVERSALITY OF EMOTIONS?

Dove Real Women campaign (2008)
(tinyurl.com/doveRB)

In 2008 Dove unveiled its "real women" advertising campaign. Using the same mechanism as HSBC's "point of view" airport campaign, the idea was to submit to the consumer a picture and offer him or her two different, and of course opposite, interpretations of it.

Famous visuals included an overweight female asking if she was "outstanding?" or "oversized?", and a white-haired lady in her seventies asking if she was "gray?" or "gorgeous?"

But no matter how clever the creative idea and how good the execution, the ad still needed textual cues to limit the number of different interpretations and ensure a common understanding of what a "real woman" was for Dove.

Nike World Cup campaign (2010)
(tinyurl.com/Nikerooney)

Contrary to the Dove example, Nike's 2010 World Cup campaign – portraying a shirtless Wayne Rooney daubed with the cross of Saint George across his arms and chest – could afford a total absence of words. The message to be conveyed to the public was the emotion of the image itself.

2. Emotions are reactions

An emotion has several properties of a reaction: an identified provocation (*meeting a bear in a forest*), an intense, conscious and short response (*chills down your spine*) and a subsequent behaviour (*running away*). As a matter of fact, the experience of emotions is for the most part inescapable and uncontainable, whereas the expression of emotions can be controlled. Again, this is notable as it means that the savvy emotion generator has a tremendous power;

the emotion receiver is unable to adapt quickly to block their approach. We have already mentioned how deeply emotions are wired into our brains, which is both an advantage and a weakness. The reactive nature of emotions, which derives from the fact that they go through less cognitive filters in the brain, has not been studied or used at all by business, marketing or communication specialists, but it is one of the key ways in which emotion-based communication can bypass the eyewalls of modern consumers.

To follow the trail of our music benchmark, the hearing of music only happens when sound waves hit our *tympanum*, which itself sends messages to the brain as a function of its perception of these vibrations.

3. Emotions are revealing

As a reaction, an emotion is a personal state rather than a quality of the person or object that causes it. An emotion does not provide information about the environment, but reveals how the environment affects someone. Hence, whilst exposed to the same match, supporters of the winning team will enjoy a much more positive experience than supporters of the losing team.

This means the emotional impact of a promotional message is a function of the environment/consumer interaction at a point in time. So any measure of the impact on consumers has to be monitored specifically, just like marketers already monitor their cognitive, attitudinal and behavioural responses. Indeed, measuring consumers' emotional reactions provides marketers with immediate insight about what consumers feel about their products, about what the mere evocation of a brand evokes to them.

The effect of music helps us understand this better: no two people ever respond to the same piece of music in quite the same way.

4. Emotions are independent of thoughts

In a pivotal paper for the history of psychology, Robert Zajonc demonstrated that emotions could precede and determine cognitions.[11] In other words, **feelings can govern thoughts**, whether we are conscious of it or not – and they do so in ways which we have no say over. While you will always have to understand a joke to enjoy it, freezing will always be your first reaction when meeting a bear unexpectedly. Emotions are instinctive.

As a logical consequence, if someone managed to 'crack' the way to generate emotions in their audience, or to use an emotion to convey a message, it would work universally (as said, there is no language barrier when cognition is not required to interpret), for the long term and with great effect.

Our music benchmark is useful again here. The effect of music is not a function of what you are thinking (in terms of reasoning) when you receive it.

Emotions, though, *are* dependent on other emotions; just as the effect of a piece of music on a person may change depending on what other music they were listening to earlier.

5. Emotions are trustworthy

An emotion is never false. While you can be mistaken about what you are thinking, you cannot be wrong about what you are feeling. For someone trying to convince an audience effectively, this is also immensely powerful as a much fuller embrace of the message can be achieved.

It is the same with music: you like it or you do not, but you never have the impression that your reaction is fake or somehow corrupted. It is a pure response. No one doubts their reaction to music.

6. Emotions are cerebral

Finally, **emotions are cerebral.** By providing clear-cut emotion-related brain cartographies, neurosciences contribute considerably to a better understanding of emotions and a localisation of their occurrence in the brain. Indeed, the first contribution of these affective neurosciences was to significantly refine the investigative fields of emotions in the human brain, identifying a group of areas habitually activated during emotional experiences. Consequently, emotions can now be defined as the result of the activation of an articulated combination

"If someone managed to 'crack' the way to use an emotion to convey a message, it would work universally, for the long term and with great effect."

of specific brain areas and neurotransmitters. We are, then, at the beginning of a revolution for our understanding of emotion-based communication. New studies will increasingly help us to understand how the brain generates and processes such messages, and the longer-term influence they have (especially the depth and purity of the message's storage).

As per our musical analogy, it is obvious to all of us that we are more sensitive to music when listening at certain periods of time, in certain environments. This has been recognised in the use of architecture and colours in music halls, which are meant to facilitate the musical flow though our ears, ultimately improving our emotional experience.

Examples of such recent scientific discoveries include a study by Zak, Stanton and Ahmadi (2007), who showed that a molecule called oxytocin, a mammalian hormone that operates chiefly as a neurotransmitter in the brain, could hugely affect what psychologists call 'perspective taking' (seeing things from a perspective other than one's own) and specifically increase the generosity of people by 80% (compared to a placebo).

The marketing and business implications of such knowledge are immense – imagine the effectiveness of a fund-raising campaign if you knew when or how a peak of oxytocin in the brain might be achieved.

Understanding the science of emotions

The following paragraphs will help us understand how emotions are born in our brains. This is a first step towards their actual 'use' for business purposes.

Since an emotion is a reaction to an external stimulation, the initial step in understanding the neuronal (or nerve cell) side of an emotion is to locate its entry points in the different areas of the brain which receive external stimulations, namely: the parietal (*touch*), temporal (*hearing*), occipital (*sight*) and prefrontal (*taste and smell*) lobes.

These sensorial lobes translate external stimulations into electrical sequences and transfer them to the thalamus, a paired structure sitting very near the centre of the brain, whose function it is to redirect them to the appropriate cortex area, i.e. the one that will provide the appropriate behavioural, cognitive or affective response to these stimulations. In the case of emotions, the thalamus will redirect the corresponding stimulations to the amygdala, an almond-shaped group of nuclei located deep within medial temporal lobes.

The role of the amygdala is to 'read' these sensorial stimulations and to translate them into emotional signals, conferring a primary role in the processing and the memorisation of emotions to this substrate. Finally, the amygdala activates the hypothalamus – the brain area that governs emotional behaviours – to trigger the appropriate emotional response.

As this organisation shows, the amygdala is at the heart of numerous emotional processes occurring in the brain. It acts like a computer processor, translating what our senses capture into a usable signal for the hypothalamus. That said, the amygdala is not activated consecutively by every stimulation. Instead, it is activated only by the limited amount of stimulations that pass through our *sensorial* filters in charge of touching, hearing, seeing, tasting and smelling.

Not quite a magic button

We can already feel the excitement of business people discovering that the amygdala is the centre of everything, the 'magic button' they have to press to manipulate consumers. But, just as you cannot manipulate a microprocessor by simply sitting in front of a computer, it is important to understand that communication will never be able to reach and influence the activity of the amygdala itself. Emotional communication will happen when the brand stimulations pass through consumers' sensorial filters and reach the thalamus, with an electrical sequence containing both an emotion and a branded message, leveraging *in fine* the amygdala's reactions. The key to getting access to the amygdala in the case of marketing is to appropriately wrap your message in emotion. We go into the detail of how to do this in a later chapter ('Feeding the message', page 79).

What the amygdala will do with this information remains highly personal, and closely related to what the consumer esteems valuable.

EMOTIONAL BLIND SIGHT

Damages to the visual cortex may cause a peculiar disability called *blind sight*. Despite reporting an inability to see objects, patients suffering from blind sight keep the ability to respond to them. In other words, despite being physically unable to see, your brain keeps 'seeing' visual stimulations.

A recent study by de Gelder & Hadjikhani (2006) demonstrated that two patients suffering from a similar brain disability were able to sense and interact with emotions portrayed in pictures presented to their blind sides. These results are extremely interesting as they indicate that we can recognise the emotions of others without necessarily seeing them, through an unconscious mechanism of identification.

While it has been initially observed as a consequence of brain damage, extensive evidence suggests that it might occur in fully functioning brains as well...and therefore plays a significant role in marketing and communication. Indeed, such a dissociation between what you think you see – *or do not see* – and what your brain actually sees may well determine all these very common, low-involving consumption situations, where you want to move quickly and appropriately, without spending time and energy thinking about it.

This has an interesting implication for marketers: it shows that low-involved consumers can *unconsciously* consider someone else's emotional reactions – those of the salesperson, of the recipient of the purchase act, of their friends, etc. – when deciding what brand or product to buy.

2.3 How to represent emotions in an actionable way

Having seen some of the key features of emotions for marketing, we also need to know how to represent and analyse them – what the 'grammar' might be for talking concretely about emotions we want or do not want consumers to experience.

A deep dive into psychological literature reveals two traditional approaches to representing the emotional phenomenon in an actionable way: the discrete and the continuous approach.

The **discrete approach of emotions** is based on the identification of a limited number of fundamental (or primary) emotions. According to the discrete view, an emotion is considered 'fundamental' when it is localised in a specific neuronal substrate, i.e. when it comes with universal facial expressions and well-defined behavioural consequences. In 1977, the psychologist Carroll E. Izard put forward a list of ten primary or 'discrete' emotions, out of which, like primary colours, all others could be formed.

Although intellectually appealing, this approach presents fundamental limitations as recent neurological developments question the idea that specific emotions rely on individual neuronal substrates. In the absence of any specific emotional substrate, Izard's assumption of basic emotions appears severely compromised.

A more viable alternative actually predates Izard. In 1974, American psychologists Albert Mehrabian and James Russell offered a different actionable approach to emotions: **the continuous approach**. This view suggests that every emotional response may be represented according to the three dimensions of PAD: Pleasure, Arousal and Dominance.

The dimension of *pleasure* – or *valence* – refers to the positive or negative, pleasant or unpleasant, nature of the considered emotion. However, despite the fact that this dimension allows a good representation of one's emotional state, it is not sufficient to allow for the differentiation of similarly disposed emotions, such as anger and sadness. *Arousal* – or *intensity* – does allow for this differentiation by revealing how intensely an emotion affects the individual. Finally, *dominance* completes this tri-dimensional representation of emotion by expressing the feeling of control one might have over one's emotions (or the situation or stimulation giving rise to them).

THE CONTINUOUS VIEW OF EMOTIONS

How to differentiate the negative emotions of fear and anger using the three dimensions of the PAD:

Fear: P- A+ D-

Fear is an unpleasant emotion (**P-**), that can be particularly intense (**A+**), which is felt because of an event the individual has only little control over (**D-**).

Anger: P- A+ D+

Anger is an unpleasant emotion (**P-**), that can be particularly intense (**A+**), whose nature leaves the choice up to the individual to confront, ignore or escape the event that causes it (**D+**).

From a research perspective, the continuous view of emotions is relevant when studying the consequences of overall emotional reactions, rather than a particular emotion. This approach to emotions allows for the measurement and the representation of the entire spectrum of emotional states, irrespective of their nature.

Considering the limitations of the discrete approach and the possibility offered by the continuous approach to separately assess emotional intensity and valence, Mehrabian and Russell's work is often considered the most practical and actionable measure and representation of emotions, from both a research and a managerial perspective.

In terms of market research, it means that emotions can be measured or at least approximated. Emotions are not simply a volatile, impalpable concept, but something real, something measurable, and not only with qualitative methods. Quantitative methods can be used to measure emotions and assess their effects – with a satisfying degree of precision – on consumer behaviours. For instance, pictorial assessment techniques such as the self-assessment manikin or the product emotion monitor index (Desmet, 2004) directly measure the intensity and the valence of a person's affective reaction, by asking him or her to circle the human face that looks like his current affective state (a sophisticated version of emoticons, in fact). Furthermore, technologically advanced tools such as facial expressions analysis, electromyography (measuring muscles' and nerves' electrical activities) or electroencephalography (measuring electrical activities in the brain) allow a more precise – yet more intrusive – measurement of human emotions.

We will not go into a full parallel between the impact of music and the continuous view of emotions, but it is easy to perceive how different kinds of music can produce different sensations, and how it is possible to define them, e.g. sweet relaxing pieces like Mozart's little night music vs. highly rhythmic pieces such as Strawinsky's firebird – with millions of possible variations.

2.4 The growing place of emotions in modern societies

"Psychology and humanity can progress without considering emotion...about as fast as someone running on one leg."

– Russell, 2003

Since the very first stages of evolution, emotions have been an integral part of human beings. In Darwin's evolutionary theory, emotions were even at the heart of the process of natural selection, as the strongest species were described as those who managed to live in groups, avoid danger and escape threats. He was pretty clear on this point: "It is not the strongest of the species that survives, nor the most intelligent, but the one most responsive to change." In other words, surviving species were those who used their emotions to cope with their environment: escape danger when frightened; widen their eyes to have a more comprehensive view of the situation when surprised; move towards a prey when reassured.

However, today's consumer no longer uses his emotions in the same way as his pre-*homo sapiens* ancestors did. Nowadays, fear is only rarely used to actually escape a deadly danger, no more than disgust is actually felt on a daily basis to avoid eating food that could seriously damage your health. Today's emotions are used differently: not only to help us deal with our environment, but also as a way of expressing ourselves. The growing importance of this in recent times is due to a transformation that took place in western societies in the past 50 years.

"This firework of old-fashioned testosterone combined with newly assumed oestrogen, both in emancipated women and in feminised men, introduced a new era of interpersonal communications: an era of emotional communication."

Until the 1960s, as far as emotions were concerned, inhibition prevailed. The 'beauty' of the emotional revolution we present hereafter is that it has comprehensively superseded this, creating the room for more self-conscious and sceptical consumers. And they are consumers that need to be talked to differently.

Historical background of an emotional revolution

Before the sexual revolution of the 1960s and 70s, in broad terms gender roles were clearly defined: men occupied public and professional circles, while women dedicated themselves to private and domestic concerns. While notions of authority, responsibility, strength and any other serious and important matters defined masculinity in the time before this, femininity was restricted to intimate spheres, with passivity, fragility and emotionality forming the cornerstones of the so-called female identity.

It was the epoch – blessed for some – of the infamous, "It's time to leave, darling, we men have to talk."

But then came women's emancipation and in its train a number of significant changes in most modern societies. In their quest for political rights and equality, women became more confident and started to enter public life. The gap between genders was increasingly bridged: women made traditional masculine values their own, and men substantially modified the way they behaved. The former took on ruthlessness, ambition, leadership, and the latter increasingly valorised and opened themselves up to a more feminine universe; one which consists of interiority, psychology, welfare, self-care…and emotions.

This firework of old-fashioned testosterone combined with newly assumed oestrogen, both in emancipated women and in feminised men, led to the disintegration of western societies' monolithic models and introduced a new era of interpersonal communications: an era of emotional communication.

This sociological evolution has been accompanied by a significant shift in psychological paradigms (ways and categories of thinking about the human mind). After the domination of the behaviourist tradition (see Pavlov or Skinner's conditioning theories), a cognitive approach to mankind evolved during the 1950s, which likened the human brain to a computer: individuals act in a rational way by gathering data and pondering its importance to make a satisfying choice. However, in the 1970s, people began to understand that the pure, cold, mechanical logic of the cognitive model was not able to explain humanity to a satisfactory degree since, as suggested by Daniel Goleman (1997), it is in our *affects* that our humanity is the most apparent. As a consequence, psychologists progressively turned their attention to the affective fundamentals of people's lives, leading to an *affect revolution*.

A change reflected in advertising

Though not fully harnessed by advertising (hence this book), this revolution is nevertheless something that can be seen already having an influence on the development of marketing over the past 100 years.

The changes in Kellogg's adverts over the years provide a striking example of this, demonstrating neatly the move from behaviourism to cognitism and at last to the affect revolution.

E.g.

Behaviourism

Started in 1913 with John Watson.

Main authors: Pavlov, Skinner, Thorndike.

The human spirit is a 'black box', which means that behaviours can be described and analysed scientifically.

A young girl holds a bowl of cornflakes and says to her mother, "Mother, guess you'll have to open the other package of Kellogg's."
Kellogg's ad (1910)

tinyurl.com/Kelloggs1910

Cognitivism

Started in mid '50s.

Main authors: Chomsky, Bandura, Schacter.

Thought is all about processing information. The human brain is compared to a computer and decision making is modelled as a step-by-step, iterative rational process.

The box takes centre stage, with the line: "It gives you food energy! Vitamins! Minerals! Proteins!" A "big-city...reporter" offers her testimony in the corner.
Kellogg's ad (1951)

tinyurl.com/Kelloggs1951

Affect revolution

Started in the '70s.

Main authors: Tomkins, Zajonc, Ekman.

Affects and emotions are the essence of both our inner balance and our social interactions.

The jaws of a nutcracker are fastened round a piece of cereal, with just the words: "Very crunchy nuts".
Kellogg's ad (2005)

tinyurl.com/Kelloggs2005

1910s

1950s

1970s

The three different Kellogg's adverts here actually leverage three different persuasion tricks:

1. the first one suggests an action: "Mother, guess you'll have to open the other package of Kellogg's" (behaviourism)

2. the second one rationalises the act of consumption: "It gives you food energy! Vitamins! Minerals! Proteins!" (cognitivism)

3. the third one actually says...nothing! It's just about triggering people's reactions (affectivism).

From intellectual intelligence to emotional intelligence

There is no single form of intelligence that can explain both personal and professional success. Instead, human intelligence can cover a wide range of disconnected abilities, going from verbal skills and mathematical capabilities to space appraisal, physical mastery, musical talent...and what the psychology of emotions describes as the use of personal or *emotional intelligence*.

According to American psychologists Lisa Feldman-Barrett and Peter Salovey (2002), emotional intelligence covers five main abilities which help us interact with others, analyse social intercourse and resolve conflict. These five abilities are as follows:

1. **Understanding your emotions**: the ability to identify your emotions – i.e. self-consciousness – is the cornerstone of emotional intelligence. Concretely, it means being able to put a (correct) word on what you feel. We saw in the Preface how difficult this is, and why we even needed proxies and benchmarks for that purpose. Someone who is blind to his feelings is at the mercy of his feelings.

2. **Controlling your emotions**: the ability to adjust your reactions to any situation relies on a proper understanding of your emotions. People who do not have this fundamental psychological ability constantly struggle with negative feelings. Those who do possess it can deal much better with life's setbacks and misfortunes.

3. **Auto-motivation**: controlling your emotions means that you are able to postpone the satisfaction of your desires or to repress your impulses. By enabling concentration and self-control, this ability is at the basis of accomplishment.

4. **Perceiving other people's emotions**: empathy – another ability based on self-consciousness – is the central element of interpersonal intelligence. Indeed, empathetic people are more receptive and sensitive to subtle signals that indicate the needs and desires of others.

5. **Mastering human emotions**: maintaining good relationships with others relies, more than anything else, on our ability to deal with our emotions. It means being able to give the priority to what you feel when it is appropriate and to allow our feelings to take a back seat when it is necessary.

In our day-to-day lives no form of intelligence is more important than emotional intelligence. It allows us to make the right social choices: establish friendships, find a personal as well as a business partner, and discover our place and role at work. Hence, as proposed by Daniel Goleman, any conception of human nature ignoring the power of emotions will emphatically lack any real insight.

IQ VS. EQ

Intellect is often assumed to be the crucial factor in success. Intelligent people supposedly triumph in everything, or almost everything, they undertake – and are natural leaders over those less intelligent, who do whatever is asked of them without question.

Fair enough. But what about the rankings of the most successful or influential people in the world, which clearly show that today's business gurus and moguls are not always those who were once bright and neatly combed students? Does being book smart make you street smart? Can you be successful with a limited emotional intelligence?

Intellectual intelligence has always been measured by IQ, but whilst most of us have completed an IQ test very few know what 'IQ' really is. IQ is a score that reflects your cognitive abilities, such as the ability to learn, solve logical problems or to apply knowledge in a given situation. IQ is thus an indicator of how good you are at solving problems…on a piece of paper.

However, things usually become more complicated when a human factor is introduced; dealing with peers can be much more complex than solving a logical problem. In this case, your intellectual skills are useless if you remain blind and deaf to yours and other people's emotions. This is precisely where emotional intelligence – measured by EQ – comes in.

EQ measures your ability to use emotional skills such as empathy, intuition, creativity, stress management, leadership and any other skill which can shape your relationships with others. Thus, as defined by Daniel Goleman, the components of emotional intelligence are those that help you to cope efficiently with dynamic human environments.

According to these definitions of IQ and EQ, it seems that emotional intelligence supports intellectual skills in any situation. In a business negotiation, for example, emotional intelligence will help you to control your initial emotional reactions so that it will not obscure or anesthetize your capacity of judgement and allow you to take the most advantage of your IQ. This is the only way to take the appropriate decision in a tense and critical situation.

Emotional recruitment

American psychologist Howard Gardner distinguished two dimensions of emotional intelligence: intrapersonal and interpersonal intelligences. In his book *Frames of Mind: The Theory of Multiple Intelligences*, Gardner described **intrapersonal intelligence** as the understanding of yourself, knowing who you are, how you react to things, what your limits are and how to push them further. People with intrapersonal intelligence are usually excellent at looking into their mind and understanding their own emotional states. As such, these individuals tend to be highly reliable as they are not involved in any self-consuming and exhausting inner struggles. Therefore, intrapersonal intelligence is your ability to draw an accurate picture of yourself and use it to drive your life.

In comparison, **interpersonal intelligence** refers to your ability to understand others, who they are, what they want, what they feel, how they work and how to interact with them. At the heart of interpersonal intelligence lies your aptitude for perceiving and reading others' emotions, in order to react in the most appropriate way. People with interpersonal intelligence are usually extroverted folks, extremely good at building relationships, since they can read and understand the emotions, motivations, desires and intentions of those around them.

"Oddly, professionals involved in marketing and communication are not required to excel in interpersonal intelligence, although it should be the raw material for their job."

People with a high level of interpersonal intelligence are good at understanding verbal and non-verbal communication. They know when controlling their emotions is necessary and when expressing them is useful and appropriate. In short, people with interpersonal intelligence are the best at communicating.

Strangely enough, professionals involved in marketing and communication are not required to excel in interpersonal intelligence, although it should be the raw material for their job. Whether being at a mainstream multinational and targeting millions of customers, or in a business-to-business environment, they should be gifted with high interpersonal intelligence, adept at building a virtual relationship with the community of their customers: feeling what they feel, being able to sense what will resonate in others' brains, and what will appeal or repel to them instinctively.

However, there is no place for the evaluation of interpersonal intelligence in the processes used by human resources departments or head hunters who hire those in the marketing industry. The main focus is on the academic background (a proxy for rational intelligence) and on previous experience (a proxy for the ability to deliver a service). Obviously the interviews will help with the assessment of interpersonal intelligence, and more often than not a candidate will not be selected because someone 'did not feel' him/her. In larger organisations this can even lead to difficulties, as the processes used by human resources will spot the candidates that tick the most boxes, and a team leader or potential future colleague having to explain why one is rejected despite this will find it rather painful – in essence, trying to rationally justify something emotional.

> **"Communication was not unemotional before; emotional benefits were simply less relevant to marketers and consumers than practical benefits and prices."**

This interpersonal intelligence is the cornerstone of what marketing and communication should be: understanding other people and being understood by them.

We are more the child of our time than the child of our father

A direct consequence of the affective revolution was to give more importance to emotions in the pursuit of our inner balance and more substance to our interactions with others – no matter what our ancestors showed us.

Emotions are now considered an asset rather than a weakness, and that is why they have become more salient in our lives. By their effects on our thoughts, our behaviours and our interactions with others, emotions are a vital force, which drive each and every aspect of our life, whether socially or as consumers.

As an essential asset for every 'modern being', emotions form this non-verbal interface between the individual and his environment, allowing him to deliver a message – sometimes unintentionally – when words are missing, inappropriate or forbidden.

And naturally, as for any other form of communication, emotions can also help to express something that is not believed, or disguise one's intentions. Indeed, the way someone expresses his emotions can differ both in width (hiding his joy, emphasising his sadness) and in nature (to feign happiness) from the reality of his emotional experience.

In other words, emotions are the very basis of human communication.

Taking everything into account, the combination of neuro-scientific, psychological and sociological considerations we have developed in this chapter emphasise the new role given to emotions in modern societies: enduring emotions is a weakness, using them is a strength...particularly when it comes to communication.

Communication was not unemotional before; emotional benefits were simply less relevant to marketers and consumers than practical benefits and prices. And just as emotions have always been there, there has always been a part of emotion in communication. But emotions have taken on a greater importance in day-to-day, interpersonal communication since the 1970s; and we have seen the appearance of an 'emotional communication', a form of communication where emotions are used as a medium and as a message.

This affective revolution has opened the door to a new way of communicating, in which emotions are a currency used much more frequently than one would think.

SUMMARY

Key actionable facts about emotions

- The *experience* of emotions is for the most part inescapable and uncontainable, whereas the *expression* of emotions can be controlled. The savvy emotion generator has a tremendous power; the emotion receiver is unable to adapt quickly to block their approach.

- Emotions are instinctive, and occur effectively 'outside' of thought: so they work both universally (there is no language barrier when cognition is not required to interpret), as well as for the long term and with great effect.

- Emotions cannot be 'false'. While you can be mistaken about what you are thinking, you cannot be wrong about what you are feeling.

- We can be objective and verifiable in our emotional marketing approach. New scientific studies will increasingly help us to understand how the brain generates and processes emotional messages, and the longer-term influence they have (especially the depth and purity of the message's storage).

- The continuous view of emotions shows us that they can be understood and targeted as a configuration of pleasure, arousal and dominance.

- In the wake of cultural and sexual revolution, societies have become increasingly emotional; across both sexes a sociological fusion of testosterone and oestrogen prevails in the form of *emotional communication*. This is an 'affective revolution'. Emotional intelligence is, or ought to be, at the heart of all marketing endeavours; it is already at the heart of many successful cultural and business icons (à la Apple, Red Bull and others), whether appreciated or not.

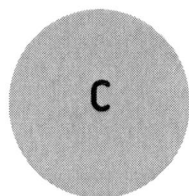  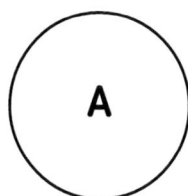

 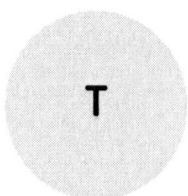 

 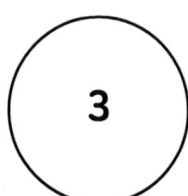

" The affective system is the primary motivational system because without its amplification nothing else matters, and with its amplification, anything else can matter... "

– Tomkins, 1984

How Emotions Matter to Consumers

What would the world be without emotion? A world where none of the people or objects around us evoke even the simplest emotion? A world with no surprise, no amazement, no shame or pride? A world where every decision, every action is the result of a cold-blooded cost/benefit decision-making process? A world without music?

Would it even be worthwhile to live in such a non-affective world?

Without emotion, i.e. without the ability to react and interact with our environment, the world would be a colourless, flavourless, soundless – not to mention senseless – succession of scenes and conversations with limited meaning. Without the hidden power of emotions, our relationships with our environment and fellow creatures would resemble those of a black and white, mute, 2D movie.[12]

As we uncovered in the previous chapter, emotions give sense to our lives, be it in private, as professionals or as consumers. But if more and more people agree on how crucial emotions are in our private relationships (and increasingly in our professional activities), less is said about how they affect consumers' lives.

Yet, as through the work of the amygdala they help to discern what is good from what is bad, what is enjoyable from what is detrimental, what is inspiring from what is boring, emotions constitute a rich set of references and guidelines for the consumer. Without necessarily dwelling on the idea of hedonistic consumerism – the continuous quest for self-gratification, for products or services that, in the mere as well as specific act of consumption, confer a kind of sensory pleasure – there is a range of evidence that shows that the lives of many consumers are simply a pursuit of happiness.

Indeed, while a utilitarian consumption pattern may help to satisfy Maslow's physiological and safety needs, research in marketing shows that more affectively-driven consumption patterns are necessary to satisfy belonging, esteem and the need to fulfil one's talent and potential.

There is a gut feeling amongst marketers and communicators that consumers might be more receptive and sensitive to experiential cues and visual performances than mere product benefits and (discounted) prices; but they lack the underlying principles for using them. And they have very few guidelines.

Since marketing and communication are serious matters – where creativity and execution should rely on a robust understanding of the consumer, his expectations, constraints and social context – clearly an organised set of information about emotions is paramount to properly handle this new form of communication. As far as emotions are concerned, there is no reason for intuition to be more important than knowledge and reflection; we have seen already that this is an area where objectivity and empiricism are eminently possible.

This chapter will demonstrate and illustrate *why* and *how* emotions are so important in the lives of today's consumers.

3.1 How emotions drive our consumer life

Emotion-driven behaviours have been a topic of interest if not for marketers then at least for marketing academics for the last 30 years. The multiple facets of the emotional phenomenon have proven to be extremely useful in explaining a vast array of consumer behaviours.

In-store behaviours (reaction to packaging features, impulsive buying), personal selling (showing empathy, reassuring the customer), customer services (dealing with customers' scepticism, anger or deception), loyalty programmes (from simple 'buy ten get eleventh free' to miles schemes or club cards), media communication (reaction to online and offline ads) and off-media communication (reaction to sponsored events, buzz marketing operations), and more, have all been addressed by researchers through an affective lens. Their findings have now reached a fascinating as well as practicable level of understanding.

An exhaustive review of the different contributions of emotions to the lives of consumers is obviously beyond the scope of a single book. Instead, we have chosen to look at those that relate to probably the most important and common marketing topics.

The fact that consumers will always be sensitive to low prices, good value for money, or the best deal possible should be unquestionable. The cheaper – *all things being equal* – the better; everybody knows that. But what we want to

> "Anyone making purely rational cases with their marketing not only misses the point but misses a range of exciting marketing opportunities."

show in this chapter is that this is, in fact, plainly untrue, and that anyone making purely rational cases with their marketing not only misses the point but misses a range of exciting marketing opportunities.

Emotion and consumption: the new pursuit of happiness

"In 99.9% of cases, all things are *not* equal."

"The cheaper – all things being equal – the better"… what a mistake!

Firstly: in 99.9% of cases, all things are *not* equal. Previous experiences of a brand and of its competitors, the context of consumption, social and communicational pressures, a consumer's mood at the time of purchase or even the weather, cannot be summarised and 'equalised' for the sake of decision making.

A consumer simply cannot put aside all he or she knows about a product or services category, or a brand, when the time comes to choose between two or more competitive products or services. They simply cannot ignore the relationships they have built; no more can they disregard the eyes of others and the social pressure that necessarily comes with belonging to and being amongst or adjacent to numerous social groups. Nor does this decrease the more important or expensive a decision is, when you might, 'logically', expect value to become even more important. When a consumer deals with highly involving decisions, such as choosing a new car, a new mobile phone or a bank, he or she is just as much, if not more, *emotionally* involved.

One of the most astonishing examples of the lack of consumer rationality is the relatively modest market share of generic medicines, as compared to original branded medicine. In Europe, generics make up only 49% of volume sales and only 17% of value sales, while they have exactly the same content and effect as the costly branded equivalents![13] How irrational are people who are ready to pay more for the very same *molecule*?

In fact, no matter how we describe an act of consumption – as the simple *satisfaction* of a given need, or as a complex compromise between financial, social or ethical constraints – each and every one of them creates an inner affective tension that engages our emotional self. That is why we spend so much time looking for *reassuring* comments on specialised forums, and talking to friends, before taking a high-involving decision; or afterwards go to great effort to *rationalise* a decision we took a bit too quickly (the universal: "Yes, I needed to buy that product. There's no harm in treating myself…").

Indeed, reassurance or rationalisation – those twin perennials of a consumer's thought process – only become necessary when the emotional self has led the way. And the emotional self is *always* leading the way.

The emotional approach of consumption, for instance, also eminently explains low-involving, automatic consumption decisions (such as toothpaste, mineral water, pasta). People tend to stick to one product or brand

> **"The consumer is perpetually in a state of emotional imbalance (dissatisfaction, envy, anxiety), that can be intense for highly involving products or services, or very mild – most of the time even subconscious – for less involving products or services."**

for these, so where is the emotional input? The point is that once you find your product you stick to it not only because it is convenient, because it prevents you from engaging in a new decision-making process, but because it spares you a new affective tension, however small.

We are not claiming that every act of consumption has the consumer plunged in an inner struggle, trying quiveringly to regain some control over his or her emotions.

Rather, the consumer is perpetually in a state of emotional imbalance (dissatisfaction, envy, anxiety), that can be intense for highly involving products or services, or very mild – most of the time even subconscious – for less involving products or services.

Earlier we used the musical comparison of two notes being slightly untuned, and creating a discomforting, inharmonious sensation, to describe the affective state of a 'feeling'. One of them has to be retuned to recreate the harmony, and thereby enable us to rebalance our emotional status. This is similar to the need for consumption, the fulfilment of which restores an internal emotional balance. **Feelings** are oriented and conscious affective states. You know what you feel, when and why you feel it and what you will have to do to restore your affective balance. *The need for consumption is nothing more or less than a feeling.* This does not make it frivolous or insignificant; indeed it is one of the most significant findings of our time.

Hedonistic canaries

"The need for consumption is nothing more or less than a feeling. This is one of the most significant findings of our time."

With the democratisation of many products (computers, cell phones, fashion designers' *prêt-à-porter* collections) and services (airlines, plastic surgery), more and more individuals have even chosen to organise their consumer lives around their emotions, to freely and in many respects consciously pare back to the purity of feeling in consumption, jettisoning much of the baggage of half-baked reason that we ordinarily build up around it.

For these hedonistic consumers, the self-gratifying, aesthetic and ritualistic dimensions of consumption and possession practices have overwhelmed the long-established dimensions of price, efficiency and robustness (Tynan and McKechnie, 2009). Unsurprisingly, this growing style of consumerism consistently shows a lack of sensitivity to traditional communications, to messages or products aimed at their cognitive brain. Instead, they respond to a more engaging, interactive style of communication, to those messages and (subsequently) products that provide them with experiential rather than utilitarian benefits.

They are pioneers.

Whether we like it or not, everything points to the rest of consumers following suit. The funny thing is that a small, if growing, group of pleasure-driven consumers have by their demands and consumption patterns given gradual rise to a new way of communicating through marketing, a way now claimed (but rarely used) by most big brands: experiential communication.

All things considered, the ultimate quest of marketers must now go beyond providing the consumer with the right good, at the right place, at the right moment and at the right price. It has to be found in a brand's ability to release the affective tension of consumption, in other words to help the consumer *feel* he or she has made the right decision. The key function of marketing is in imparting the *feeling of satisfaction* that will be provided by the consumption of a particular brand or product.

And it obviously raises an ethical concern, since the feeling of being satisfied does not always involve the consumer's genuine satisfaction. We will look at this later in Chapter 4.2.

The affective trigger: no decision without emotion

Elliot was a successful man, cherished by his wife, praised by his colleagues. But Elliot had a benign tumour in the prefrontal cortex that needed to be removed. Although the surgery was technically a success, Elliot's life would never be the same.

When he came back to work, Elliot saw his performances declining so badly that he eventually lost his job. In the meantime, a series of unfortunate financial decisions put him in a difficult economic position. And even his private life was affected: he divorced from his first wife, married another woman and divorced again. To top it all off, his insurance kept refusing to indemnify him, as no medical or neurological evidence could reveal any major pathology. Indeed, his perceptive aptitudes, his memory, his learning capacities and his linguistic and mathematical skills all seemed to be intact. Every time he was faced with a problem, Elliot was perfectly able to understand it, identifying the different possible solutions and the various consequences of each of them.

But all the problems and upsetting events he encountered since his brain surgery proved that something was going wrong: he had lost the ability to solve the problems of everyday life. This is an ability that relies on the cooperation between the frontal lobes and the amygdala (the emotional brain we described in 'Understanding the science of emotions' in Chapter 2 – see page 39). The connection had been impaired by his brain surgery. Elliot was able to understand the ins and outs of every problem he faced, but he was simply unable to make any decisions…

According to Antonio Damasio, the professor of neuroscience who helped make Elliot's case famous:

- The prefrontal cortex elaborates fugacious representations of our possible actions as the first step in helping us face the diversity of our choices.

- The amygdala then appraises these blurred pictures and attaches the outlines of a corresponding emotional reaction to each of them.

- These emotional outlines form what Damasio called "somatic markers", whose role it is to help the brain in sorting through potential solutions on the basis of their overall emotional consequences.

Hence, people suffering from a lack of connection between the prefrontal cortex and the amygdala have difficulties in integrating the emotional implications of their decisions into their decision-making process. This leads either to unwise decisions…or no decisions at all.

Elliot saw his life falling apart after his brain surgery because he had lost the ability to use emotions in making his decisions, and this prevented him from making any decisions or, by extension, sound choices.

"Elliot's sad case means a revolution in the perception of the consumer: no decision without emotion."

Beyond the illustration of another brain mechanism, Elliot's sad case constitutes a groundbreaking step in the understanding of consumer behaviours. It means a revolution in the traditionally cognitively oriented perception of the consumer. This revolution can be summarised in four words: no decision without emotion.

What Elliot's case taught us is that emotions, far from being an obstacle, are actually the *sine qua non* of decision-making, whether that decision-making is 'rational' or not. The process (problem identification, solutions proposition, consequences assessment) can be rational, but a decision itself must always involve an emotional element. Indeed, what is a decision if not the process of giving your preference to one solution over another? The act of choosing the solution that will generate the consequences you are *happier* with?

Neurology and brain imagery confirm that there is nothing like an emotional vacuum. We are in a universe which continuously provokes a multitude of affects, ranging from unconscious to goose-bumping emotional reactions. The example of Elliott shows us that there is no such thing as cold, purely rational decision-making. No matter what our level of rationality and cognition, there is simply no decision without emotion.

Emotion and creativity: the motivational power of emotions

Since the mid-nineties we have seen the development of massive collaborative marketing campaigns based on a principle first initiated by IT developers: co-creation. It is sometimes referred to as 'crowd sourcing' and is made possible by internet-based tools.

The idea behind these campaigns is to tap into consumers' expertise to develop a product, a design, a communication campaign or even to determine a price. In most cases, obviously, the consumer is financially or materially incited to participate, as asking them to do the marketer's job unpaid would not be attractive.

Famous examples of collaborative campaigns include the P&G Advisors program from Procter & Gamble: a web platform through which consumers can test new products and give their feedback, allowing P&G to reduce its usual pre-test procedures from two months to two weeks. Doritos' "Crash the Super Bowl" campaign falls in the same category: consumers are invited to submit their own ad for Doritos; the best ads, as determined by a public vote, are then aired during the Super Bowl final, with a prize giveaway for the best six, rising from $25,000 to $1,000,000.

Not only did the Doritos spots perform well in the Cymfony survey, but they came in at fifth position in the Nielsen BuzzMetrics survey of online conversations about Super Bowl ads. Both Doritos spots also finished amongst the ten most-viewed moments of the game in households that used TiVo digital video recorders to watch the Super Bowl.[14]

Beyond their benefits in terms of CRM (customer relationship management) and brand image development, collaborative campaigns are interesting precisely because they rely on a highly emotional process: creativity. Indeed, despite often being described as an intellectual combination of supposedly non-related thoughts leading to the production of new ideas or concepts, research shows that creativity is predominantly influenced by affects and, in particular, emotions. This has importantly fruitful implications for modern marketers.

THE SCIENCE OF EMOTION

A recent paper from Baas et al. (2008), examining the results of 66 studies dealing with emotions and creativity, concluded that the emotional state of a person affects his creativity, especially when it comes to emotional valence (whether the emotion is positive or negative).

From an evolutionary perspective, positive emotions are reassuring enough to incite us to explore, build relationships with others, and develop our knowledge and experiences, whilst negative emotions make us focus on possible threats. In other words, whilst positive emotions broaden our attention and allow us to see the whole picture, negative emotions narrow our attention and help us deal with immediate problems. Obviously, as far as creativity is concerned, one would prefer a panoramic view rather than a porthole!

Positive emotions, then, aid creativity.

However, the relationship between emotions and creativity might be a bit more complex, according to recent neurological findings. A study from Rowe et al. (2007) concluded that positive affects not only broaden the scope of outer and inner attention filters but also reduce their selectivity.

Hence, by weakening our inhibitory defences, positive affects allow us to allocate more attention to both external and internal cues. Therefore, positive affects will help us to use more cognitive material to feed our creative process (attention scope); will allow us to consider more elements as relevant to the problem we wish to solve (cognitive scope); and will boost our cognitive flexibility, increasing the probability that diverse cognitive elements will be associated to form a creative thought. Seeing the world through rose-tinted glasses may not just be a metaphor anymore – converging evidence suggests that affective states are associated with changes in attention, perception and cognition.[15]

The practical consequences of these results give the idea that a happy consumer will not only be a good spokesperson for your brand – there is nothing new about that – but also, and foremost, a creative one. Hence the utility of empowering and involving them in the communication of brands. They will not replace an advertising agency in meeting the usual strategic needs, but will certainly provide the brand with brilliant ideas (as they do not have any creative barrier) when – and if – they are given a good reason to do so. This is the beginning of a virtuous circle; creative engagement is emotional engagement, which begets greater creative engagement and greater emotional engagement – and so on, potentially *ad infinitum*.

On a more anecdotal note, we often hear happy consumers being creative about the products they support: Apple fans will convince you their laptops are faster, Toyota customers that their cars are

"A happy consumer will not only be a good spokesperson for your brand, but will certainly provide the brand with brilliant ideas if they are given a good reason to do so."

flawless (even after massive recalls), powder-baby-milk users that they will have healthier children, Verizon clients that the network is more resilient, Levi's jeans fans that they last longer, etc. This is all untrue, either in absolute terms or relative to some competitors at similar prices. As consumers become fans – and unconsciously try to maintain their emotional balance on the topic and justify their decisions to the outside world – they invent qualities and benefits that products or brands have never had. Quite the dream situation for those in charge of promoting them…

When even cash becomes emotional

Back to our chapter about rationality, the approach of economists – and even 'good sense' – tells us that a buck is a buck, and there could not be anything less emotional than a buck.

To challenge this assumption, we would like to look at two findings of Harvard Professor Nicholas Christakis and University of California Professor James Fowler, as detailed in their book *Connected*. They came about from tests using game theory.

The first test is the 'Ultimatum Game' and works as follows:

- Player 1 is given $10 to split with Player 2, however he or she wants.

    - If Player 2 accepts the split, both players get their part.

    - If Player 2 rejects the offer, both players get nothing.

Theoretically, Player 2 should accept any split, since something is always better than nothing!

But most offers under $2 are rejected by Player 2.

The second one is called the 'Dictator Game' and is the following:

- Player 1 is given $10 to split with Player 2, however he or she wants.

- Player 2 *must* accept the possible offer (this is why it is called the Dictator Game…)

- Both players get to keep the money.

Theoretically, you would expect Player 1 to keep all $10, since his or her own economic wellbeing can be entirely satisfied without Player 2's consent; the latter has no possibility of declining an offer of $0.

But experimental results indicate that Player 1 often allocates money to Player 2 regardless, reducing de facto the amount of money he or she receives.

● ● ●

Such results are astonishing. This research shows that money is not approached by humans in a cold-hearted, purely logical way. However strange it may seem, we have a complex of feelings towards the coins in our pockets or balance on our bank screen. It is not the kind of bonding we have with a newborn baby, but nevertheless the use of these coins or notes, their meaning, our perception of their role and value, is inextricably emotional – and must therefore differ entirely depending on the *emotional context* we are placed in.

From an economic viewpoint it creates a serious problem in most quantitative theories, as the very basic currency that balances the different market forces is more plastic than that. If supply is higher than demand, the axiom runs that prices decrease to reestablish the balance…but of course they do not if consumers are sufficiently stressed or excited; the market might be numerically flooded, but not emotionally exhausted. In effect, the currency used in the mathematics of market demand can have different values or meanings depending on the audience's mood or moods.

From a communications and marketing viewpoint, it means even the most enduring rationality-based promotions (BOGOF, 50% off, cashback/rebate) could be improved, depending on the emotional context of consumers. Their efficiency, at present, is not questioned – but the perceived 'value' they offer to consumers ought not to be taken for granted as a job well done. Their potency will vary with the emotional context of the consumer and the emotional appeal of the marketing. A whole component of making such campaigns as successful as possible has therefore largely been ignored, or addressed only inadvertently.

THE PERCEIVED VALUE OF MONEY

Would you rather earn £100,000 when everyone around you makes £50,000, or make £200,000 when everyone around you makes £400,000 (for the same job, with no difference in terms of living costs)? In other words, do you prefer to earn a smaller amount of money but still more than others, or a bigger amount of money but still less than others?

A rational choice would be to choose the second option, as it is obviously better to earn £200,000 rather than £100,000 (with no difference in living costs and no difference in the demands of the job). But in reality, as surprising as it sounds, most people choose the first option: being richer than other people, but less rich than they might otherwise be!

For some scientists, this experiment clearly demonstrates the irrationality of man. But we rather think this experiment shows something more interesting: in essence, as with the game theory findings earlier, that money is not an emotion-proof concept. There, first irrational greed and then irrational generosity impinged upon the decisions of participants, who had nothing financially to gain from such reactions. And here we see that the perceived value of money can be biased by irrational forces such as self-perception, sense of social rank and notions of fairness or injustice.

In particular, do not underestimate the last of these. A brain imaging experiment by Sanfey et al. (2002) showed that unfair offers activate several brain areas, particularly the anterior insular cortex, a region connected with visceral disgust.

This salary experiment is important from a marketing perspective because it illustrates that the consumer's unwillingness to accept unfair offers is as much an emotional as a rational reaction. Current practice of addressing the customer's sense of fairness through purely rational arguments ('Great deal!' 'Sensational savings!' 'Guaranteed bargain!') is therefore, in many respects, rather senseless – or at least missing several tricks.

3.2 The '3 Ms' of emotional communication: mindset, message and mechanic

Just like any other form of communication, emotional communication cannot be considered independently from the receiver's mindset. As we said before, the consumer is always in a state of emotional imbalance, and always seeking acts of consumption and rational justifications that can restore that balance. Indeed their emotional state might evolve at any moment because of the communication itself and at any point during the communication.

This modification of the consumer's emotional state will unavoidably impact the way he or she will process the message: from a superficial consideration, to a deep and precise elaboration of its content.

"Emotional communication is the ultimate form of communication. It fully addresses the multifaceted way in which audiences receive and respond to communications."

The beauty of emotional communication is that it can be seen as the ultimate form of communication. This is because emotions are not only part of the message communicated by the brand, they also determine the consumer's mindset when he or she receives the message and the way he or she will process it. It fully addresses the multifaceted way in which audiences receive and respond to communications.

Shaping the mindset: emotions and our senses

All of the information that surrounds us is collected by our sensory organs and transferred to the cortical regions of the brain, to be processed and then fed into our decision-making. Emotions are central to this process precisely because they translate what our senses capture into more-or-less appropriate reactions, allowing us to position ourselves in our environment. Therefore, in most cases, our senses trigger our emotions.

That said, all senses should not be considered equal; some of them are far more frequently and potently solicited than others. For instance, the senses of sight, hearing and touch are continuously sought – one cannot prevent oneself from seeing, hearing or touching – whilst we can breathe without smelling any odour and swallow without experiencing any taste.

We saw in the beginning of this book the huge amount of visual data our brain has to process; 34 gigabytes a day, including a lot of promotional messages. We also saw how, clearly, we cannot allocate our attention to each of these pieces of information, particularly when it comes to visual stimulations. Naturally, therefore, we oppose a filter to this mass of information – the eyewall described earlier – which helps us consider only what is relevant to us. We also suggested that leveraging customers' emotions might offer a way of circumventing the eyewall, slipping through it – thus thwarting these perceptual defences. How?

It is precisely the multi-sensorial nature of emotions that is the most effective way to trick the eyewall.

Most obviously it means that communications can get through by using several senses to convey the same message to consumers' brains, or different bits of the same message which their brains then recombine. But firstly and perhaps most importantly, *it sets the terms of interpretation*.

Setting the terms of interpretation through multi-sense experiences

Of course, whilst it is natural to combine the visual and aural senses (in televisual advertising, for instance), it is always difficult to go further with more senses. Nevertheless, since multi-sense is probably the ultimate emotional efficiency, and since modern marketing is decreasingly bound by '2D' media, we will analyse a few examples of common multi-sense experiences.

The key thing that will emerge is that they help to illustrate how effectively coordinated multi-sense experiences determine the overall context in which messages or information reach audiences; and that this context is more than half the battle in persuading an audience to both listen and to take to heart whatever it is you are trying to say.

Stendhal syndrome

A striking example of the power of a multi-sensorial emotional experience is the so-called 'Stendhal syndrome'. Named after his visit to Florence in 1817, this syndrome is a psychosomatic illness described by famous French novelist Stendhal in the following terms:

"As I emerged from the porch of Santa Croce, I was seized with a fierce palpitation of the heart; the wellspring of life was dried up within me, and I walked in constant fear of falling to the ground."

Italian psychiatrist Graziella Magherini recorded over 100 such cases in tourists and visitors to Florence in the mid-20th century, and, as the name suggests, the phenomenon goes back to at least the 19th century. This peculiar syndrome illustrates the sheer power of emotions (provoked in this case by multi-sensorial experiences of all the art on display in the Uffizi) on ourselves, on our physical and psychological balance – even against our own will or knowledge.

Sports games

Attending a sports game is also a multi-sensorial emotional experience, and one of the strongest and most common that people experience today.

It involves a mixture of hearing (songs, rhythms), physical feelings (vibrations of fans jumping), viewing (the game itself, supporters' materials and choreography, images on giant screens) which creates a distinctive affective experience for those attending. It is an affect made even more intense by dint of imbuing a feeling of relative uniqueness in those present: 'I am amongst the few that are physically here, personal witness to these dramatic events, whilst millions didn't have any other choice but to watch it on TV.'

When you exit the stadium you have a vague and pleasant sensation of being rather exclusive; the people you meet in the street who attended have an immediate affectionate (or perhaps antagonistic) bond with you, as fellow parties to a mutual and by definition enclosed experience; those you meet who did not attend, on the other hand, seem different, less desirable humans.

People who go to music festivals or concerts also experience highly similar emotions during and after the event. Such impressions fade quite quickly, of course – good news for the stability of our societies.

Naturally, sports institutions and event organisers have over time increased and refined the visual, physical and aural attractiveness on display before, during and after games in order to increase the audience's emotional experience to the highest possible levels. The most prosaic top-tier football match is now framed at the venue by thunderous music from recent exciting films, by cutting-edge graphical displays, by sponsored flag days and numerous other affective adjuncts – the more critical matches, indeed, by firework displays, flames bursting from the ground and celebrity mini-concerts. Some stadia are built on giant shock absorbers to enable fans to jump without risking the foundations collapsing.

It is now normal to find specialised TV producers appointed by major sport events, and charged with ensuring the live occasion produces the most exciting broadcast possible: the one that conveys the biggest 'quantity' of emotions. The rules of baseball were partly developed for similar reasons in times past, and today even cricket has been substantially modified under the Twenty20 format to optimise and concentrate the public's emotions – as well as making the games more TV friendly. During the 2010 football World Cup in South Africa, a ban on the vuvuzela (a plastic horn that produces a one-note drone – one of the top searched words on Google in 2010) was mooted by media and sports representatives, as their intense noise *en masse* was upsetting players and commentators. FIFA rightly decided to let them stay, as they were part of the experience, both for spectators and for TV viewers. Aurally as well as in terms of authenticity, the instruments contributed to the uniqueness and intensity – and therefore the emotional value – of the whole affair.

The same kind of *emotionalisation* of the experience is taking place across other less likely cultural venues and events, too. Recent developments in museum practice have challenged the conventional idea of a silent, motionless temple of art or history. Modern museums increasingly offer interactive, multi-sensorial experiences in an attempt to better engage visitors – think of the hidden ceiling speakers, touch screens, overlapping displays and lighting effects, the video, text and audio hybrids offered by the Churchill Museum (2005) in the Cabinet War Rooms, London, all of which sit alongside and around conventional glass cases with immobile exhibits. Thanks to a livelier multimedia context, such museums offer not only a richer experience but stronger memorisation – beyond seeing, now learning by living, by confrontation, by directing our own investigations into the matter on offer. Beneficial to visitors, it also improves cultural access without compromising on the quality of the artistic or factual content.

E.g.

MODERN MUSEUMS: FROM EXHIBITION TO EXPERIENCE

With its Art After Dark programme, the Guggenheim Museum of New York has set up one of the most original multi-sensorial museum-based experiences. On the first Friday of most months, the ground floor is taken over by a friendly and fashionable crowd dancing to the music of well-known DJs. And, of course, if at some point during the evening you want to have a look at the paintings and installations, you'll be more than welcome to leave your drink behind and head up to the galleries upstairs.

Another great example comes from the British Music Experience at The O2 arena in London, where visitors can play on Gibson guitars, Slingerland drums, Baldwin digital pianos, and even a vocal booth sponsored by Sennheiser. Following instruction on a touch screen, visitors receive step-by-step video tuition from real recording artists who show them exactly how they play their songs. They can download their gigs later via the internet.

Who said that a museum should be silent and boring?

All this works because, as research in persuasion shows, an assimilation effect can be formed between what the consumer feels at the time of their exposure to a message or event and what they feel about the message or event: a message received in a positive mood, in a richer emotional environment, will be better memorised and more appreciated than the same message received in a negative or mild mood.[16]

What the senses capture from an environment is critical, as it shapes the mindset in which the consumer will receive the message.

Therefore, before questioning themselves about the best message to express, communicators should seriously think in terms of the *context* of exposition. The main consequence of consumers' over-exposure to communication is that they are more and more sensitive to the communication context, and less and less aware of messages that approach them from unfavourable ones.

Feeding the message: emotions and brand knowledge

When it comes to remembering an event, a person or an object, American psychologist Robert Zajonc demonstrated that the affective content of the memory is usually the first characteristic to emerge. We remember through our emotions. As such, both the storage and the recollection of a message relies on its embedment within a network predominantly of affective references: personal relevance of the message, emotions felt *during* the message, emotions felt *because* of the message, and so on.

In other words, the affective context of the message is memorised together with the message itself, in what psychologists call an associative network of memories. The emotions wrapped up with the message become part of the message in the individual's memory. At the end of the learning process, retrieving the message will trigger the corresponding emotions, whilst retrieving the emotions will ease the message recollection.

In the light of the motivational power of emotions and their centrality in making any decision, this idea of affectively-charged memory networks takes on great importance when it

"A message received in a positive mood, in a richer emotional environment, will be better memorised and more appreciated than the same message received in a negative or mild mood ."

comes to communication. There is much to be gained by a brand keying in its communications, messages or marketing operations to what we might call an *affective label*, as it will ease the memorisation of the marketing, make the brand more accessible in consumers' minds at the time of purchase, and enhance its longer-term appreciation.

E.g.

LINKING COMMUNICATION TO AN AFFECTIVE LABEL: THE CASE OF COCA-COLA

The 2010 FIFA World Cup was an excellent opportunity for Coca-Cola to convey its global marketing campaign – Open Happiness – through the world's most popular sport. How they went about doing so is a great example of a brand attaching itself to a pleasing affective context rather than attempting just to directly communicate with consumers.

The South African event saw the soda brand launch a "What's your celebration?" promotion, an invitation for audiences across the world to devise, perform and upload their own dramatic football celebrations in order to win prizes. It declared that it was inspired in this by ritual dances many African players perform when they score a goal, a practice introduced by Cameroonian football legend Roger Milla, ambassador of the campaign, in the 1994 World Cup – and since adapted into unique routines by countless European and South American players.

Through this individual promotion Coca-Cola was not directly selling its drinks, nor the benefits of drinking them. Rather than advancing a message, it invited consumers to partake in the passion and happiness conveyed by football players themselves. They, too, could be part of the spontaneous, worldwide euphoria surrounding the tournament.

In practical terms, Coca-Cola deployed an integrated multimedia platform – including a promotional component (collector cans, reproducing the campaign's graphical identity), a media component (dedicated advertising spots, and a 60-minute documentary recounting the best goal celebrations) and an interactive component (an online competition allowing consumers to post their own celebration videos, from which Coca-Cola then made a video clip).

The showstopper was the awarding of the Coca-Cola World Cup Celebration Award to the player who invented and performed the most popular goal celebration during the competition, as voted for by consumers. Millions fans worldwide chose South African Siphiwe Tshabalala as the most iconic goal celebrator of the World Cup.

"What's your celebration?" was a clever and affective way for Coca-Cola to reach consumers. Through this campaign, their communication was clearly embedded within an emotional, celebratory context; one that was both relevant to their brand (Open Happiness) and that reached out to and included their consumers. Coke reinforced its association with happiness and happy moments in consumers' minds, in large part by inviting and enabling them to be happy.

Research in psychology, consumer behaviour and neurosciences all leads to the same conclusion: memorisation is always better when the input to be memorised is strongly connected with an emotion. The reason is that the amygdala – the 'emotional brain' – directly modulates the activity of both the hippocampus and the prefrontal cortex, two regions highly involved in memorisation. These three regions act together to improve the retention of emotionally exciting events and ease their long-term recovery.[17]

Hence, the persistence and the accessibility of an event or a message in the memory is strongly linked to the individual's emotional experiences.

THE EMOTIONAL NETWORK OF MEMORIES

Still reluctant to consider the strength of emotionally led networks of memories? How about a little homemade memory test: ask yourself the following two questions:

1. Can you remember what were you doing – and where – on the 2nd of February 2002?

No way – that was a long time ago!

2. Now, can you remember what were you doing – and where – when you first heard about the 9/11 attacks?

Most of us can remember pretty easily what we were doing, and where, when we first heard the terrible news. One of the authors was checking his emails in a Nepalese internet café, while the other was working in London, on the phone, trying to speak with an HSBC bank branch next to the Twin Towers, and (unaware of what had just happened) calling the unhelpful employees names as they were not picking up the phone...Like most people, they will remember these tiny details all their lives.

You might say there is little actual memorisation going on in being able to remember an event mentioned across the media, history books and society. Yet if that were the case, why would we remember more trivial, personal elements such as where we were and what we were doing at that time? We remember that day and those details because all the terrible pictures, footage and testimonials immediately aired forged a rich (for want of a better word) emotional context. This emotional context means the memorisation of every element more or less related to an event.

In conclusion, regardless of why a brand's communication is stored in consumers' minds, the emotional context in which the communication was received is always stored in the same network. Hence consumers will associate brands with an emotional response in their memory, and over time this will mean better memorisation and more (or less) favourable attitudes towards those brands. The less emotional their experience of the communication, the less remembered it will be.

So this is something over which marketers can and must seek to have greater accuracy and awareness than at present.

Defining the mechanic: emotions and information processing

Over the last 30 years, research in marketing has consistently demonstrated how emotions affect the way consumers process commercial communications. It has also stressed the fact that the impact of emotions cannot be properly addressed without separately considering the two dimensions of emotional intensity (strong vs. weak) and valence (positive vs. negative).

Hence, two different – yet potentially interdependent – mechanisms have been proposed to explain the influences of emotions on communication: the intensity principle and the processing efficiency principle.

Intensity principle

According to the *intensity principle*, intense emotional reactions tend to focus a consumer's attention and cognitive capacities on the precise element provoking his emotions, to the expense of the treatment of more 'peripheral' elements.

The benchmark with music is helpful again here. Anyone can feel the different levels of immersion in the listening experience depending on how much one likes it, how good the interpretation, how favourable the environment. Sometimes it seems all of our brain, spirit and heart is focusing on the music; sometimes we are scarcely even distracted from another activity.

This explains why, while a very emotional TV programme might overshadow the ads that run in its breaks (since they are peripheral to the source of emotions), an emotional advert that runs in the breaks of a neutral programme may well catch the consumer's attention and deliver its message in the best conditions possible.

"Moderate emotional intensity is best, as it allows an optimal level of memorisation."

This perhaps helps explain why funny ads, sexually suggestive ads and ads involving babies (or puppies) are popular for an astonishing range of products – they have a better chance of standing out against whatever the programme they are run against, as a kind of emotional shout over the affective noise.

When applied to the context of sport sponsorship, the same intensity principle leads to very surprising, though in some respects not contrary, results: the more emotional the game, the poorer the memorisation of the sponsors whose logos actually surround and appear in the action continuously.[18] Focusing on the very reason for their emotions (the action, teams, players, score), supporters are able to ignore even what is printed in vast letters across the players' chests and flashing at them the length of the football pitch on billboards.

HOW DO EMOTIONS AFFECT THE MEMORISATION OF SPONSOR BRANDS?

Originally developed by psychologists Robert Yerkes and John Dodson in 1908, the Yerkes-Dodson law established a relationship between arousal and cognitive performance. The law dictates that cognitive performance (such as memorisation) increases with physiological arousal (conceptually similar to emotional intensity), but only up to a point. When levels of arousal become too important, performance decreases.

This relationship is often described as a curvilinear, inverted U-shaped curve which increases and then decreases with higher levels of arousal.

Applied to the sponsorship context, and given that sponsorship persuasion takes place in a dual task situation (the consumer receiving sponsors' messages while watching a game), one should expect that low levels of intensity would be insufficient to draw attention and prevent consumers from adequately processing the sponsor's message. Likewise, excessively high levels of intensity would also distract the audience's attention away from the sponsor's message. Hence, one would anticipate an inverted-U shape relationship between emotional intensity and brand recall in the context of sponsorship, and that people with a moderate level of emotional intensity would report an optimal level of sponsors' memorisation.

Research conducted during 2008's French Open grand slam tennis tournament confirmed that spectators' emotional intensity and sponsors' recognition are correlated. Emotions felt by spectators in the stand do affect the memorisation of the event's sponsors (Bal, 2010).

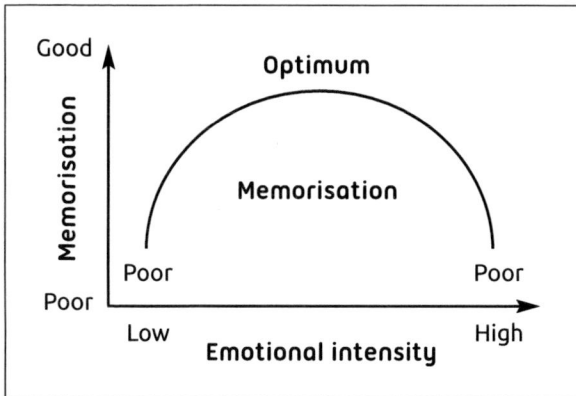

Image first published in Bal C., Quester P. et Boucher S. (2007), Emotions and Sponsorship Marketing, Admap, Issue 486, pp.51-52.

This research also confirmed that the shape of this relationship was the one described by the Yerkes-Dodson law, with an inverted-U shaped curve. Hence, moderate emotional intensity is best, as it allows an optimal level of memorisation.

All in all, the consequences of this intensity principle are neatly summarised by Vennetier (2005), who explained that at times "emotion blinds us; not as a black veil thrown in front of us but rather as a light projected directly into our eyes, preventing us from seeing the rest of the picture". This is critical knowledge for brands that are trying to convey their message alongside separately emotionally rich experiences: such marketing needs to be carefully judged to avoid being hidden from the consumers since the 'light' is too strong.

Processing efficiency principle

Another posited, though not necessarily competitive, emotional mechanism relies on the *processing efficiency principle*. Rationales for this mechanism are pretty straightforward: people tend to process information more efficiently when they are in a positive mood rather than a negative one.

This is directly linked to the motivational power of emotions we described in the previous section 'Feeding the message: emotions and brand knowledge' (page 79), according to which a positive mood helps broaden and deepen the repertoire of thoughts and concepts one might use to process a message. Consequently, when the consumer is in a good mood, his or her processing of the information leads to a more elaborate encoding, storing and (later) restitution of the information. Inversely, a consumer in a bad mood is more preoccupied and might not consider the advertised brand or – worse? – will process it regardless of the message the brand initially wanted to convey.

Again, when applied to sport sponsorship, the processing efficiency principle helps us understand the impact of sport-related emotions on sponsorship effectiveness. Whilst exposed to identical stimulations (same game, same players, same perimeter boards, etc), jubilant supporters from the winning team will show a better memorisation of sponsors and a better understanding of their presence, than will the demoralised supporters of the losing team.[19]

Whether you consider them separate or connected, these two active principles clearly show that emotions affect not only brand memorisation – which, as we all know, is an antecedent to the sacrosanct brand awareness – but also higher stages of brand understanding: brand attributes, brand knowledge, brand images, brand values and so on.

However, these two principles also suggest that the different effects of emotions on brand communication are not as simple and straightforward as one might think. In truth, if it is widely acknowledged that emotions can significantly enrich a brand's communication, they can also easily overshadow or harm it.

3.3 From one to many: emotional contagion and mirror neurons

We have seen that the emotional context in which the consumer receives a message should never be ignored. However, can we generalise what is true at the individual level across a group or a whole population? What happens when, instead of facing a brand's communication alone, the consumer shares the experience with others?

To answer these questions, Hatfield, Cacioppo and Rapson (1993) suggest the notion of emotional contagion, which they describe as "a tendency to mimic and synchronize facial expressions, vocalizations, postures and movements with those of another person and, consequently, to converge emotionally". Hence, when people are in a certain mood, that mood is often communicated to others. Talking to someone who is depressed may suffice to make us feel low, and talking to someone ecstatic can be enough to make us feel good.

Evidence of emotional contagions have been found in animal research (monkeys can catch the fear of other monkeys and make appropriate avoidance responses), in developmental research (infants react to the pain of others as if it were happening to themselves) and in clinical research (therapists are constantly struggling with themselves to keep a sufficient emotional distance from their clients).

DISTANCE, WHAT DISTANCE?

Nicholas Christakis, a social scientist at Harvard University specialising in health and social networks, initially researched if a personal health condition could be influenced by, or could influence, the social network(s) in which one lives.

Using obesity as a research field, his findings showed that if your friends are obese *your* risk of obesity is 45% higher. And if your friend's friends are obese, *your* risk of obesity is still 25% higher. Most remarkably, if your friend's friend's friend – someone you probably do not even know! – is obese, *your* risk of obesity is still 10% higher. And it is only when you get to your friend's friend's friend's friends, that there is no longer a relationship between that person's body size and your own body size.

Christakis and other researchers have also shown that this astonishing contagion effect extends to non-concrete elements such as political allegiance and happiness. The latter, in particular, explains why some cities or regions in the world are known to benefit from an atmosphere where relationships and projects are easier. This is the case of Rio de Janeiro, Sydney, Barcelona or Amsterdam (according to a Forbes 2009 ranking of the world's happiest cities). This has nothing to do with a sort of an invisible force somehow leading people to better personal and business practice, but is the result of a positive feedback loop whereby once a sufficient number of helpfully disposed people and businesses exist in one place, solution and help begets solution and help; and a naturally self-perpetuating process of business improvement is initiated and accelerated – effortlessly.

Frighteningly, the same holds true for areas experiencing serious problems.

This tendency to take on other people's emotions has played a central role in relatively recent history. Indeed, emotional contagion has been a key lever in most political propaganda, where one-sided messages were created and presented to the masses in order to produce an emotional rather than rational response, and therefore modify attitudes and behaviours in line with a political agenda. Furthermore, and notwithstanding their legitimate economic and geopolitical causes, one cannot help but notice that emotional contagion played a great role in most modern conflicts, infusing as it did a common emotion across a people: enmity and resolve during World Wars I and II, depression during several economic crises, fear during the Cold War and after September 11th.

And what has proved to be true with negative emotions has also worked with positive emotions. For instance, when the French national football team won the 1998 World Cup, held in France, not only did feelings of pride and enthusiasm spread across the entire population (horizontal propagation) in a social capacity, but they also filtered through the different layers of the country (vertical propagation) and their respective individual concerns: politicians celebrated the success of the multicultural French ideal, brands discovered the formidable marketing potential of French players, bankers rubbed their hands looking at stock exchange rates, whilst happy supporters rediscovered the ecstasy of frenetic consumption. What happened in France has also happened elsewhere, as demonstrated by ABN-AMRO's 'Soccernomics 2006'. This study showed that, from 1970 to 2002, winning countries have benefited from an average extra growth of 0.7% the year following their victory at the FIFA World Cup.

How can this emotional contagion be explained? Explanations about our ability to convey emotions from one to another may be found in an extremely promising area of neuroscience: mirror neurons.

Initially discovered by a group of Italian neurologists led by Professor Giacomo Rizzolatti, mirror neurons represent a distinctive class of neurons, localised in the ventral premotor cortex and the rostral part of the inferior parietal lobule. The fascinating particularity of mirror neurons is that they activate identically both when we execute a motor act and when we observe another individual performing the same or a similar motor act. In other words, it means that your brain reacts similarly when you do something and when you see someone else doing the same thing – when you celebrate a happy moment *or* witness someone else being happy, part of the brain's activity is absolutely identical.

According to Indian neurologist Vilayanur S. Ramachandran:

> "the discovery of mirror neurons is the single most important 'unreported' story of the decade. […] [M]irror neurons will do for psychology what DNA did for biology: they will provide a unifying framework and help explain a host of mental abilities that have hitherto remained mysterious and inaccessible to experiments."

At the same time as mirror neurons provide the scientific framework for the efficiency of non-advertising communication (i.e. everyday conversation, socialising, life), they also explain the efficiency of marketing campaigns that might target lots of little audiences – that seek not so much to bombard everyone, in the hope of reaching someone, but do all they can to make intimate connections with a number of people or groups, sometimes referred to as 'tribes' (and their marketing use as 'tribal marketing').

The mirror neurons are the missing link for the propagation of messages between such receiving individuals or groups and their friends, friends of friends and so on. This natural resonance of ideas and experiences, spreading messages from brain to brain, in a partly unconscious or subliminal way is an extraordinary discovery, and – like much that we have seen in this chapter – still to be leveraged by marketers.

"Mirror neurons explain the efficiency of marketing campaigns targeting lots of little audiences"

SUMMARY

The emotional consumer

- Emotions constitute a rich set of references and guidelines for the consumer; more affectively-driven consumption patterns are necessary to satisfy belonging, esteem and the need to fulfil one's talent and potential.

- In 99.9% of cases, all things are *not* equal when a consumer is weighing up purchase choices. They simply cannot put aside the web of associations – built from previous experiences of a brand and its competitors, the context of consumption, social and communicational pressures, their own mood, etc – that comes with contemplating a purchase.

- The consumer is perpetually in a state of emotional imbalance (dissatisfaction, envy, anxiety), that can be intense for highly involving products or services, or very mild – most of the time even subconscious – for less involving products or services.

- The ultimate quest of marketers must now go beyond providing the consumer with the right good, at the right place, at the right moment and at the right price. It has to be found in the brand's ability to help the consumer *feel* he or she has made the right decision. The key function of marketing is in imparting the *feeling of satisfaction* that will be provided by consumption of a particular brand or product.

- Creative engagement is emotional engagement, which begets greater creative engagement and greater emotional engagement – in a continuous virtuous circle.

- Addressing the customer's sense of fairness through purely (or largely) rational arguments is in many respects senseless.

- Emotional communication fully addresses the multifaceted way in which audiences receive and respond to communications. Emotions translate what our senses capture into more-or-less appropriate reactions.

- Effectively coordinated multi-sense experiences determine the overall context in which messages or information reach audiences; and this context is more than half the battle in persuading an audience to both listen and take to heart whatever it is you are trying to say.

- The emotional dimension of a message is memorised together with the message, and both aid the recollection of each other. There is therefore much to be gained by a brand keying in its communications, messages or marketing operations to what we might call an *affective label*, as it will ease the memorisation of the marketing, make the brand more accessible in consumers' minds at the time of purchase, and enhance its longer-term appreciation.

- For brands that are trying to convey their message alongside separately emotionally rich experiences (e.g. through sports sponsorship), such marketing needs to be carefully judged to avoid being hidden from the consumers because of the too intense emotional experience. The same holds true for emotionally impoverished experiences.

- Emotions affect not only brand memorisation – which, as we all know, is a consequence of the sacrosanct brand awareness – but also higher stages of brand understanding: brand attributes, brand knowledge, brand images, brand values.

- As consumers become fans – and unconsciously try to maintain their emotional balance on the topic and justify their decisions to the outside world – they invent qualities and benefits that products or brands have never had. Quite the dream situation for those in charge of promoting them…

- There is now neuroscientific support for, and increased understanding of, the efficiency of marketing campaigns that target lots of little audiences – seeking not so much to bombard everyone, in the hope of reaching *someone*, but doing all they can to make intimate connections with a number of people or groups, from whom the communications can then spread by a social and neurological process involving mirror neurons.

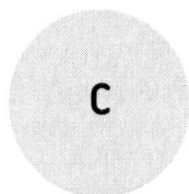 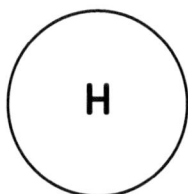 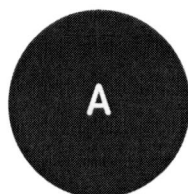

 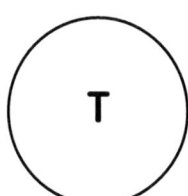 

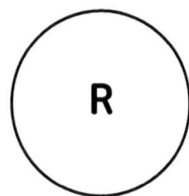 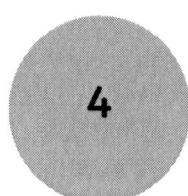

" Any emotion, if it is sincere, is involuntary. **"**

– Mark Twain

Emotion, the Holy Grail of Brands?

S o far, we have learned what an emotion is (Chapter 2) and why it is so important for the consumer (Chapter 3). With this in mind, we can now change our perspective – from the communication receiver to the communication transmitter – and build on these insights, addressing the issue of emotions from the side of the brand and the marketer.

How do you effectively use emotions in communication? What risks have to be avoided when using emotions in communication? What ethical issues are related to the use of emotions in communication?

We will address these questions in the coming pages.

4.1 Emotion-enabled communication techniques

In this section we are going to study some relatively well-known communication techniques that rely on messages being embedded in or with emotions, but which do so at present without bringing to bear the kind of detailed systematic knowledge about emotions and the consumer now available to us (Chapters 1-3) – and the artlessness of which can and should, in future, therefore be refined. We will be looking, indeed, at suggestions for exactly how to do so.

These communication techniques include celebrity endorsement, sponsorship marketing, product placement, experiential marketing, user-generated content and (in some aspects) corporate hospitality.

Celebrities are a source of emotions for their fans

Long after the first celebrity endorsement – Pope Leo XIII's official approval of Vin Mariani in the 19th century (a patent medicine containing cocaine) – the support of cultural icons has become one of the most widely used communication techniques. The use of celebrities in communication platforms has been on a constant rise over the decade 2000-2010, reaching truly vertiginous figures, with over $3bn invested in 2009 to secure celebrities' rights; 25% of all American ads involving celebrities in one fashion or another; and up to 70% in Japan doing likewise.[20]

Thankfully, it (sometimes) works. For instance, the $12m, three-year contract which Chanel signed with Nicole Kidman in 2006 – and the memorable ad directed by Baz Luhrmann – helped the brand increase its Chanel n°5 sales by 30% (according to Euromonitor).

Reasons for such success are related to the celebrity's ability to make a brand's message stand out, to heighten brand recall and awareness, to convince consumers of the credibility of a brand's offerings, to generate a transfer of values from the celebrity to the brand, to shape brand identity, to attract new audiences, to create a loyal attachment, to mobilise public opinion and to express a complex positioning that is otherwise hard to convey. A celebrity can be a usefully subtle or impressionistic symbol.

In other words, celebrity endorsement to some extent covers many of the key potential elements of emotional marketing and communications that we established in earlier chapters.

Consumers do not purchase celebrity-endorsed brands because of the utilitarian implications of that endorsement. The 'seal of approval' it confers, the implicit suggestion that if the product is advertised by *x* it cannot be iffy, is largely neutralised today by the ubiquity of celebrity involvement in marketing and the cynicism of the modern consumer. The real contribution of celebrity endorsement is to help the brand become more embedded in the consumer psyche – crucially, with the opportunity it provides consumers for self-expression, self-realisation and self-identity.[21]

Consumers use endorsed brands both to find and to assert their place in their social environment. This idea was humorously illustrated, but no less embodied, by Apple's famous *"I'm a Mac"*, *"I'm a PC"* campaign.

Thanks to his or her own personality and accomplishments, a celebrity brings to a brand or product a collection of meanings, values and emotional episodes (for instance from movies or concerts) that instantly evoke feelings in the consumer. And by combining these characteristics with their brand, marketers expect a transfer to occur from the celebrity to the brand; and for consumers to find this alluring, not least because they too can receive a transfer from the qualities of the celebrity. The magic can also rub off on them. Their self-expression, realisation and identity can partake of that of a well-known or respected public figure.

But whilst celebrity endorsements depend on a number of the crucial emotional aspects of successful communication, this is largely guided, at present, by intuition. A lot of attention is, of course, paid to finding a celebrity that somehow best embodies a brand (or what a brand wants to be); but very little is paid to the ins and outs of emotions and how a celebrity-endorsement campaign might best leverage them. This can lead to expensive missed opportunities.

There are many ways for a brand to use a celebrity. We have developed a typology of celebrity endorsements. It is based on the *depth* of emotional association that is achieved between a brand and a celebrity in a marketing campaign (or range of campaigns), and this is determined by the level of involvement that the celebrity is deployed at in the campaign. We identify four basic levels, in ascending potency:

1. Brand face
2. Brand ambassador
3. Brand contributor
4. Brand collaborator

1. Brand face: featuring the celebrity exclusively in an ad campaign

This is the case, for example, with Eva Mendes for Revlon, Maria Sharapova for TAG Heuer and Sean Connery for Louis Vuitton. They are simply pictured together with the product they have endorsed.

Such campaigns are usually a one-off relationship, and typically strike audiences as a purely commercial relationship devoid of much in the way of sincerity or honesty. Communications that use this low level of involvement vanish from the average consumer's mind almost as soon as they see them.

Instead of using a blank canvas and trying to show a nice advertisement to their target audience, 'brand face' endorsement uses the one-dimensional emotional ploy of juxtaposing someone well-known with a particular product – and no more. It hopes to attract attention and increase the penetration of the brand or message into the audience's brain. But if you were to replace the celebrity with an unknown face how potent would its impact be? Exactly. So just how badly are they missing out on the possibilities? Well, precisely!

The rationale behind it is that any marginal extra attention that a famous face can bring will increase awareness for the brand and, in turn, the efficiency of the advertising campaign. As it is delivered in bulk to millions of targets, any small percentage change of buying behaviour from the targets can result in a significant sales uplift.

Strangely enough, these 'brand face' contracts are often referred to as *endorsements* of the product, service or brand by the celebrity, but in reality they are not endorsements at all. Although most celebrities would not feature in adverts for a brand they despise, the fact that they agree to play a role for a few seconds or for a picture is not an endorsement. And everyone knows it. With celebrities under constant scrutiny, most of the audience see straight through such arrangements. This is especially true if the audience only sees the association between the brand and celebrity in commercials, and nowhere else (special events relayed by the press, for example). The public feels that the touch points between the celebrity and the product are minimal, confined simply to the ad. The result is that the emotions conveyed by the celebrity only marginally benefit the advertiser. There is a limited transfer between the two, and this prevents the brand from fully benefiting from the potential power of the partnership with the celebrity.

Furthermore, these kinds of practice may actually leave a bitter aftertaste. Internally there is often some resentment about these campaigns; the brand's employees can feel the celebrity has been paid an awful lot of money for little personal investment in the success of a brand or product, quite the stark contrast to their own case of serious personal investment and comparatively minor remuneration.

2. Brand ambassador: the celebrity becomes a spokesperson and appears in PR and corporate events

Well-known examples of this are George Clooney for Nespresso or L'Oréal's "égéries" (see the next example). It is a much deeper relationship than just using an image in a 30-second ad or for a print ad; the celebrity is not merely juxtaposed with a brand, but personifies it across a range of media and for a long timescale.

This includes the use of their image in advertising, but also public appearances at special events, contributions by the brand to a charity supported by the celebrity, a 'spontaneous' (though usually specified in the contract…) mention of the brand in a press interview as something they care about, and much else besides.

E.g.

PORTFOLIO OF CELEBRITIES: L'ORÉAL'S ÉGÉRIES

L'Oréal *egéries* (muses or spokespersons, in English) offer an interesting example of celebrity endorsement. Far from the simple 'brand faces' we described earlier, the particularity of L'Oréal egéries strategy is to have cleverly reproduced the variety of its marketing segmentation – in terms of ethnicity, age and gender – into a portfolio of celebrities.

Rather than monolithic and universal brand faces, the celebrities are meticulously chosen and featured according to their origin.

This greatly facilitates the self-identification process between the consumer and the celebrity. Hence, the Latin-American actress Eva Longoria is present in campaigns for American and European markets, while Freida Pinto (*Slumdog Millionaire* heroine) endorses the brand in the Indian market, and Cheryl Cole in the UK only. Thanks to L'Oréal, each consumer group has it own muse.

L'Oréal deploys the same strategy when marketing an anti-aging skin care, with the brand using a mature celebrity (such as Andie MacDowell or Jane Fonda) to promote this range of products.

Within a category of similar products (for example, foundation), L'Oréal will also simultaneously engage several celebrities from different ethnic origins. In this way, the cosmetics giant supports the diversity of its offering within a category of certain products and reassures its customers by showing that they can provide the right product for everyone.

L'Oréal egéries is therefore what we might call the first 'variable-sweep wings' endorsement strategy. Depending on the country, the targeted consumers and the product being promoted, L'Oréal's portfolio of celebrities is deployed (singly and multiply) in careful coordination.

Whilst each individual contract does not go as far as a brand ambassadorship, the synergistic accumulation of all the égéries and their use in ads and high-visibility events (such as the Cannes Film Festival, sponsored by L'Oréal), creates serious impact for the brand and generates a good return on investment.

The next few years will tell us whether the recent endorsements of L'Oréal products by Matthew Fox (in 2008), Patrick Dempsey (in 2009) and Eric Cantona (in 2010) are the successful beginnings of a similar celebrity strategy for promoting male care products.

As such, brand ambassadorship is a more sophisticated form of partnership, as it multiplies the contact between the consumer and the brand-celebrity association. Nevertheless, the level of association between the brand and the celebrity remains rather weak, as the public can still see through such agreements. It does not take too much to perceive that celebrities are being paid to attend certain parties and pretend to like a product they do not necessarily consume.

3. Brand contributor: the celebrity brings a visible, and genuine, contribution to the brand or product

Famous examples of this include Chantal Thomass, who created a line of make-up products for Nivea, Lenny Kravitz who created a song about what Absolut Vodka meant to him, and Karl Lagerfeld, who designed a ready-to-wear collection for H&M and a series of bottles for Coca-Cola Light (aka Diet Coke).

Brand contributor endorsement allows a celebrity to authentically personify a brand and/or its products. From the brand's side, the idea is to obtain a product or a communication that the brand would never have been able to create without the contributing celebrity or with another celebrity, tapping much deeper into the celebrity's credit and awareness with the public. And from the celebrity's side, beyond the financial aspects of the deal, the aim is to affirm his or her own image by collaborating with a more or less iconic brand.

At this stage, celebrity endorsement is no longer about image transfer from the celebrity to the brand, but about the celebrity's interpretation of the brand – and, therefore, something of a mutual exchange between the two.

E.g.

DITA VON TEESE AND COINTREAU

In 2007, liquor brand Cointreau implemented a celebrity endorsement strategy to generate high visibility for a spirit whose primary usage is as an ingredient in cocktails, and to reinterpret, update and personify its "Be Cointreauversial" branding in a spectacular and concrete way.

Cointreau chose American Dita von Teese (who is "cointreauversial" not only as a burlesque strip-teaser, but also as the ex-wife of a tenebrous rock star) as a global ambassador and offered her the opportunity to contribute in more depth to the marketing of the brand.

In the following months, von Teese met with mixologists to create a new cocktail, the Cointreau Teese, which was cleverly close to her personal taste (with the use of an ingredient she loves: violet). The cocktail was released over several launch nights, where Dita von Teese also performed a sensuous show she created specially for Cointreau. Internally, a movie was made about the partnership between Dita von Teese and Cointreau, in order to sell the concept to its subsidiaries and incite them to sponsor numerous local marketing operations revolving around Dita von Teese and the burlesque world that she embodies.

As a result of this partnership, Cointreau is now positioned as a dynamic and ambitious liquor brand, able to inspire other brands of the Rémy Cointreau Group to initiate their own partnering strategy with celebrities. From a commercial perspective, the partnership helped the sales team to sell more products: the demand for cocktails made with Cointreau increased. Dita von Teese appeared to strike a fine balance between brand positioning and the need to establish a firm platform for better on-trade (presence in bars and restaurants) boosting of markets.

Reasons for the success of this partnership rely on the fact that the burlesque star genuinely likes the product, worked hard with the brand to create a new cocktail and new show, took part in several events and appeared in communication materials. Consequently, every time Dita von Teese subtly mentioned her role as ambassador for Cointreau in interviews, her commitment was perceived as genuine and trustworthy.

The reason why brand ambassador programmes work better is linked to the transfer of emotions. This is exemplified in the non-advertising activities, which have to be at least as important and as visible as the simple advertising (otherwise people will see it as the more cynical first or second level of involvement). The brand benefits from the blurred perception by the consumer between the brand and the celebrity, itself derived from the strong multi-channel and multi-touchpoint links, ultimately fooling the consumer's eyewall. The consumer will have more sympathy for the brand, and will accept the messages from the brand as if they were originated by the celebrity, driving acceptance and awareness.

4. Brand collaborator: the celebrity is deeply involved in the brand's decision-making process and communications

This is the deepest relationship possible between a brand and a celebrity, since the celebrity will take an active role in marketing and communication, and even strategic business decisions.

There are only a few examples of 'brand collaborator' endorsement, one being American rapper Jay-Z, who joined the marketing board of Budweiser in 2007 to help develop their new brand: Budweiser Select. As well as appearing in high-profile events as a regular brand ambassador, Jay-Z participated in planning sessions to provide thoughts and insights on various brand programmes, and collaborate with Budweiser's agency on upcoming TV ads, radio spots and print campaigns.

Another famous example is Bruce Willis's ownership of 3.3% stakes in Belvedere, a French and Polish vodka maker, in exchange for him promoting Sobieski Vodka around the world from 2009 to 2012.

Other best practices of close collaborations include the close links between sport equipment manufacturers and their endorsed athletes. Both parties collaborate to design technical improvements to the product and to find the best ways to market the products. Recent example includes tennis players Serena Williams and Roger Federer, who designed their own lines of sportswear for Nike, based on what they need and like to wear on court.

The importance of being honest

Without necessarily going to this advanced form of collaboration between a brand and a celebrity, what is critical to the success of an evolved celebrity endorsement programme is to convey sincerity and honesty, from both the celebrity and the brand.

Large corporations usually underestimate the capacity of mass audiences to see through their communications and feel when such a programme is artificial. A study from IMAS International (2007) shows that consumers have increasingly lost their confidence in messages communicated by celebrities, with only 7% believing in celebrities' conviction for a brand or product that they advertise.

So the only way to increase consumers' acceptance of the message is to involve the celebrity more deeply in the endorsement, and to demonstrate that his or her commitment has more to do with a personal connection with the brand than anything else.

Sponsorship marketing and the 'goose-bump effect'

The origins of sponsorship marketing date back to Roman times, when patrons, including Julius Caesar, sponsored gladiatorial games. Such events were political in intent, designed to entertain the public, win its respect and thereby protect their positions and fortunes. Today, despite an estimated US$59.4bn invested in rights acquisition, with 65% to 75% being devoted to sports properties (brandRapport, 2009), the tenets of sponsorship marketing are much the same, though the forms have evolved significantly.

We define sponsorship marketing as a communication technique used to promote a company by signalling its commitment toward a non-commercial activity – which activity conveys its own range of values, meaning and emotions – in order to reach a variety of marketing, commercial, corporate and/or managerial objectives through a kind of virtue by association.

In other words, a bank sponsoring a Formula One car is trying to achieve something similar to what a clothes manufacturer aims at by using a famous actor in their ads, even though it is in some respects reversed: the sponsor appearing in the context of the sponsored, rather than the celebrity appearing in the context of the product.

The myth of values transfer in sponsorship

Most current sponsors tend to justify their sponsorship commitment by evoking – or maybe, invoking? – a community of values with the sponsored property. The transfer of the property's values to the sponsors is considered as the principal intangible benefit of sponsorship marketing (a complement to tangible ones such as tickets, number of perimeter boards or license utilisation).

> 'I want my brand to be perceived as friendly, robust and reliable. So I'd better sponsor a rugby team, since rugby is known for its values of camaraderie, physicality and team spirit. Oh, and I don't mind if different brands, from different industries, choose to

sponsor the same team, mentioning the same community of values…'

However, many academic works show that for such a value transfer to occur consciously, the following four conditions must be satisfied:

1. **Consumer consciousness**: every consumer knows that a sport event has sponsors, but it does not mean that he or she will notice or identify them.

2. **Consumer attention**: to decipher the sponsor's message, the consumer must notice it. His attention should not therefore be absorbed by something else (such as the sport action itself).

3. **Consumer participation**: the consumer has to question himself about the presence of the brand, its legitimacy at the event, and the message the brand wants to convey.

4. **Consumer learning**: for the value transfer to occur, the consumer has to know the sport's values *a priori*, before coding and storing them in his memory together with the meanings, symbols and values already evoked by the brand.

But which consumer – aside from marketers – satisfies all these conditions when he watches an NBA game, the last Formula One race of the season in Abu Dhabi or the Olympics in Beijing?

Which sport enthusiast is simultaneously conscious, attentive, ready to question himself about the sponsors and disposed to learn sponsors' messages? And ultimately, which consumer will voluntarily try to construct a connection between the sponsored property's values and those of the sponsor without being explicitly asked to do so by a market research company or a group of researchers?

As we saw, in part, in Chapter 3: probably not many. (See the inverted U-curve in 'How do emotions affect the memorisation of sponsorship brands?', pages 84-5.)

● ◦ ◦

The particularity of sponsorship marketing is to engage the consumer in a highly emotional context, based on the affective relationship he has built with the sponsored property and on the emotional reactions it provokes. For sports events in particular, the opportunity they offer to momentarily escape from reality, or to combine both the excitement and the stress of a suspenseful match, lays the foundation for an emotionally wrapped communication. As such, sport sponsorship constitutes an ideal framework to study emotions from a communication perspective: be it based on collective performances or individual achievements, a sporting event offers a wide array of emotions with a variable degree of intensity and valence to form the contexts in which the consumer receives a sponsor's message.

As a communication technique, the particularity of sports sponsorship is to address the consumer when his attention is essentially focused on a sport's show. Appearing in the periphery of the action, the sponsor's message will therefore be processed – if processed at all – by a lowly involved consumer, reluctant to allocate too much of his brain power in trying to understand the motivations of the sponsor brand, the reason for its presence or the message it wants to convey.

For that reason, the sponsorship persuasion process is often described as a peripheral, unconscious treatment of sponsors' brands, in which consumers' emotional reactions play a central role because they do not require extensive brain power.

Surprisingly, though, despite much evidence and numerous developments regarding the 'emotionality' of the sport sponsorship persuasion process, most sponsors, rights sellers and consultancies keep focusing on a more cognitive-exigent variable: sports values. But, as we suggest in 'The myth of values transfer in sponsorship' (page 107), waiting for consumers to make a cognitive connection between the sponsor and the values of the sponsored property is a dubious way of proceeding. By doing so, most sport sponsors not only have to run what neuroscience shows to be a frightening gauntlet towards genuinely impacting on the consumer. They also fail to benefit from what really contributes to the richness of what they are sponsoring: the emotional transactions happening between the property and the consumer.

E.g.

"90 MINUTES, 90 EMOTIONS" – CELEBRATING FOOTBALL EMOTIONS IN AUSTRALIA

Research commissioned by the Australian football premiership – the Hyundai A-League – revealed that both fans and non-fans were particularly sensitive to the continuously evolving atmosphere and emotional highs and lows that characterise football matches.

To market its distinctive place in the Australian sporting landscape in accordance with this research, the league launched a TV ad campaign, in 2008-09, celebrating the infectious atmosphere that comes from the emotional extremes experienced over 90 minutes of a football game.

Taglined "90 minutes, 90 emotions", the commercial depicted spectators' experiences, from the euphoria of a goal celebration to the desolation of a red card, ending with the generic vibrant energy of a crowded stadium.

The campaign was also brought to the streets of Sydney and Brisbane through the means of a simple yet bright interactive street marketing activation, whereby actors brought football emotions to life. Actors dressed as supporters were placed on pedestals with several pedals, each of them representing a specific football emotion. By pressing one of these pedals, passers-by could choose which emotion they wanted the actor to perform.

Product placement

Product placement is as old as entertainment itself, but has accelerated rapidly since the early 2000s thanks to franchises old and new such as James Bond, *The Matrix* and *Friends*. It works by having a product shown in a movie, television programme or video clip, or even in a computer game or book.

For it to be efficient, it has to be easy to see and recognise for a sufficient amount of time, and to be relevant to the action and/or character.

Famous examples include Nokia in *The Matrix*, which created a real boost for the brand for many years. Examples of the practice carried to excess include the last few James Bond movies, *Minority Report* and some TV series (*Sex and the City*, for instance).

The great advantage of product placement is the presence of the product or brand right in the middle of the action, putting it alongside the emotion generated by the entertainment.

Product placement has to be used in a very subtle manner: as usual, consumers can be quick to detect the commercial agreement behind it. If they feel it is *not* an honest and genuine partnership between a brand and, say, a movie, they will see it as an embedded (or worse, hidden) advertisement. And, having paid for the entertainment, they will not be amused. It is a rule of thumb that either the consumer accesses free entertainment paid for by advertising, or they pay for the entertainment and are reluctant to accept any advertising in it.

So along with celebrity endorsement and sponsorship marketing, product placement shares the absolute requirement of being structured as a true partnership, of imparting authenticity and realism, and not being just another form of advertising.

E.g.

I, Robot (2004) – USING PRODUCT PLACEMENT TO RAISE AUDI'S EMOTIONAL APPEAL

For the first time in the history of product placement, German manufacturer Audi created a vehicle explicitly for the fictional world of a blockbuster. The movie was *I, Robot*, and the car was the Audi RSQ. Rather than having their product intruding on the action, this kind of bespoke product placement saw the action intruding on their product: like a cocktail designed (and not just drunk) by a celebrity, here the car is effectively designed by the film. It is a true partnership, the apparent creative integrity of which forms a basis for significant emotional appeal.

Visible for a total of almost nine minutes in the film, the Audi RSQ placement proved particularly successful. Surveys conducted in the USA revealed that the concept car gave a substantial boost to the image ratings of the brand in the USA. Consumers exposed to the movie became more attached to the brand than those who did not see *I, Robot*. And the core values of Audi – attractiveness and performance – gained considerable ground among spectators.

Moreover, the Audi RSQ has not only been a marketing coup. The concept car has also influenced the design of a new road car model – the Audi R8 – introduced in the German market in 2006.

Experiential marketing

Experiential marketing is a form of communication aimed at connecting with consumers more intimately. This it achieves by addressing them on multiple levels – through their senses, emotions and behaviour – in order to bypass the eyewall.

As such, experiential marketing can be defined as the art of creating an experience aimed at connecting a brand, product or service to a consumer, using authentic and personally relevant events.

To be effective, experiential marketing has to tap into a consumer's social identity, lifestyle and ambitions. In order to do so, brands need to have a perfect understanding of the mindset of their target audiences. That is why understanding what the consumer thinks is not enough; brands have also to pay attention to their senses and feelings.

E.g.

NIVEA'S SUNNY MEN

To promote the launch of its new sun spray in 2009, Nivea created a great piece of experiential marketing with an original beach tour in France.

The pitch was simple: how to connect with female consumers and make them try the sun-protection cream in a way they will never forget? And the solution was even simpler: a group of good looking, friendly young men traveled around Atlantic and Mediterranean beaches to offer the most basic of services: massaging sun cream into female holidaymakers' backs.

Following the success of 2009 (more than €1.5m of media value), Nivea enriched the concept in 2010, asking its team of Sunny Men to also teach Sunny Classes, which taught holidaymakers how to get the perfect tan.

Based on the mirror neuron discoveries mentioned earlier (Chapter 3, 'From one to many: emotional contagion and mirror neurons', page 87), we can argue that such an experience created by a brand may not only be present in the audience that lived it, but also diffuse throughout their close circles. The message can spread exponentially.

Strangely enough, this is similar to the 'viral' effect of a YouTube video (often referred to as 'viral marketing'), which requires the amplifying effect provided by technology. This, however, operates without any laptop, iPhone or internet connection – completely naturally, using the human brain's ability to transmit emotional knowledge to other brains through mirroring.

User-generated content (UGC)

User-generated content describes the ability given to consumers to produce their own personal audio, video, graphic or text content in relation to a product and its promotion. The benefits of these were touched on in Chapter 3, in the section 'Emotion and creativity: the motivational power of emotions', (page 67). In short, neuroscience shows that creative engagement leads to emotional engagement and greater brand receptivity – and this boosts creative engagement, emotional engagement and brand receptivity – and so on…

From a marketer's point of view, there are a number of things to consider when making this as successful as possible.

Firstly, the results of UGC need to be sufficiently high quality to be worth sharing – and sharing them needs to be an easy, preferably automatic, process. Over the last five years, some brands have started using their financial power to accomplish just this – providing tools, frameworks, technical and editorial assistance to make the generation of content a real experience for their consumers.

This is precisely what appliance retailer DRL Ltd successfully did in 2010, with the redesign of its dedicated review site www.appliance-reviews.co.uk into a more customer-centric reviews hub. Rather than searching by product feature, customers can now narrow searches by consumer group to find products rated highest by people like them…with all the reassurance and positive reinforcement it conveys. Since the redesign, bounce rate has dropped by 312%, time on the site has more than doubled, page views per visitor has more than tripled, and the returning visitor rate has increased by 46%. Conversion traffic from www.appliance-reviews.co.uk has tripled to 15.1%.[22]

The internet is obviously the perfect tool for this purpose. It enables a level of automation and customisation which ensures quality and reach at the same time. This obviously includes social media, but can also take the form of humorous augmented-reality applications, such as the one offered by E.ON, a utility giant, which enabled users to hold the FA Cup (in reality they face their web cam holding a sheet of paper with a coded design, which the application transforms into the Cup). The outcome was a self-generated picture or video, which could then be shared on social media like Facebook.

Better yet, UGC can be taken to the next stage, as we see in the next example, enabling users to create not only their own promotional material – but their own (yet still branded) products.

E.g.

PETIT BATEAU'S TALKING SHIRT

In 2010, Petit Bateau – a centenary French brand of clothes for all ages emphasising good quality and soft material – deployed an excellent example of a UGC campaign.

It had an innovative and funny, even intimate, approach; and managed to match it with promoting its brand as well as immediately selling its products. It was called Talking Shirt.

The concept was simple and straightforward, and consisted of t-shirt kits that included a blank Petit Bateau shirt, 29 stamps and two washable ink pots.

Je change d'humeur comme de t-shirt was the tagline ('I change my mood as I change my t-shirt'). Petit Bateau was inviting consumers to create their own unique slogan t-shirt, adaptable to whatever they wanted to say; and to truly take control of their Petit Bateau product and what it meant to them. The consumer became brand collaborator.

This was matched with another UGC online campaign, where users could employ a Facebook app to create a video display of just such a t-shirt, with the slogan being a succession of the Facebook statuses of the consumer over the past 18 months. This

> not only demonstrated the UGC of the product, through a UGC ad, but also gave rise to a certain sense of nostalgia. The perfect emotion for such a brand.

At the fringe: the power of corporate hospitality

Corporate hospitality is not a communication technique in the strictest sense, as it is mainly an opportunity for salespeople – just as much the CEO as those working in the sales department – to entertain clients or potential clients. So it is, in truth, a commercial rather than a marketing tool. However, its advantages can also be understood by the same emotional framework as successful modern marketing; and such emotional insights should be borne in mind by corporations hoping to make it as successful as possible.

The power of corporate hospitality is to leverage an emotional moment – more often than not a sports-related one – which makes the relationship between you and a potential business partner special, enabling a form of bonding that can ultimately lead to additional business.

Entertaining someone at a cricket game, a tennis event, a NASCAR race, or an opera production – whichever may be of interest to your potential business partner – is extremely powerful. You share excitement, maybe disappointment. You may well end up shouting or crying together, being carried away by beautiful melodies or speeches, experiencing accelerated heart rates or goose bumps at the same time.

So corporate hospitality enables the creation of a form of cognitive phase between you and your guest: something they will memorise (a thousand times more than a brochure, an electronic newsletter or an ad); and something you have in common, an event you will be able to recall together in the future. It is the corporate equivalent of the multi-sense experience of, for example, the museums in Chapter 3 (see the section 'Setting the terms of interpretation through multi-sense experiences', on page 75). Barriers to communication are lowered; psychological inducements to being receptive and attentive are advanced; business discussions are greatly facilitated.

The reason why we consider corporate hospitality to be at the fringe of our topic is because it does not, per se, allow the design and conveyance of a message. Nevertheless, the importance of emotions in marketing goes to show that the selection and organisation of such events must be thoughtful, and aim at all times for the most emotionally rich experiences possible.

4.2 Careful when playing with emotions

Beyond their emotional dimensions, all of the techniques studied in this chapter so far have other elements in common. This includes a number of requirements that need to be respected in order to ensure their use is sufficiently effective and that they are integrated successfully into a platform involving other marketing and communication channels.

But most importantly, since emotional communication aims at touching the consumer in the most intimate spheres of his or her humanity, the use of emotions in communication requires a profound and diligent consideration of ethics.

These points will be addressed in the following paragraphs.

Requirements for the use of emotions in communication

We have already seen the necessity of honesty in the relationships between a brand and an emotion-carrying asset, something totally different from classic advertising or media buying which is only driven by the supply and demand of eyeballs.

A number of issues have to be taken into account to use emotions in communication cleverly and effectively. This includes taking into consideration the specific risk of emotional communication; thinking about the timing and length of campaigns; making sure that the emotional communication is properly integrated into the communication platform; and, needless to say, appropriately measuring and tracking the results.

Risks

The risks of emotion-based communication techniques mainly lie in the potential instability of the brand's emotion-conveying assets. Newspapers are full of news items that discredit celebrities, who are both life models for a portion of the population and endorsers for one or more brands. The same happens in the sports universe, where you can never be 100% sure about the issue of the game or the performance of the players. Similarly, you can always discover too late that the movie you placed your products in is a complete disaster!

This continuous uncertainty is both the magic and the drama of emotional communication, its greatest supportive argument and its biggest counter-argument. It is the reason why honesty is such an absolute requirement in emotional communication. When the celebrity does not act as the brand would like him or her to, when the sponsored team does not perform as was expected, or when the movie does not meet its target audience, the only thing that remains for the brand is the honesty of the communication intention. Research is, at present, inconclusive on this topic, but we are convinced that brands who *abandon their celebrity* after a scandal will sooner or later face a backlash from consumers. It is the proof of a fake – a dishonest – marriage, so that even if it limits the damage of value contamination from a disgraced entity, it is never without cost.

There are numerous ways to mitigate these emotional risks, and it is the expertise of specialised agencies, which do a similar job in planning and executing emotional communication campaigns as advertising and media agencies do with traditional communication campaigns. The raw material is different, the risks are different, but the end result can be as predictable.

Timing

We have all had the feeling of embarrassment when confronted with a moment that is supposed to be emotional – at a wedding, a keynote address, or an official ceremony – but which lost all of its emotional appeal because of bad timing (it was not the right thing to say, show or do at that moment) or inappropriate length (it was too quick to be really honest or so long as to be exhausting).

Every time you want to move a consumer, the best way of evaluating your appeal is to put yourself in his or her shoes. As with any other marketing tool, the rational model is of no use here: simple empathy suffices.

Would I like or need to be confronted with a particular emotion at that time? Is it an appropriate emotion to elicit given what has come before and what is coming next? Bear in mind the wider narrative that your 'chapter' or paragraph of an advert/communication will be dropping into – whether in terms of its placement in an ad sequence or on a website, or in terms of what has been happening in the wider world.

Common sense is half the battle.

A famous example of falling foul of this was a French advertising campaign for Peugeot, in 2008, designed to promote the pleasure of driving a Peugeot 207. The ad depicted a father deriving so much enjoyment from driving his car that he forgot to drop his children off at school and only realised, at the end of the advert, that they had spent the whole day on the backseat with him. The emotional appeal here is, via guilty or knowing amusement, to a mixture of self-indulgence and family feeling at the same time: just right for a carmaker hoping to reach that segment of the market that must purchase its vehicle for practicality, rather than mere pleasure, but has not resigned all ambitions of luxury.

Nevertheless, the timing was disastrous – and the bold balance between these two emotions was destroyed. The week preceding the launch of the campaign, two news items had stunned the country: two young children had died, having been left and forgotten by their parents in a car for too long.

Integration

Very often brands and corporations forget that celebrities, sports events and entertainment platforms are businesses too. When in discussions with a large brand, the objective of such entities is not the same as the brand's; they will be looking, quite naturally, to make the most amount of money with the least amount of effort.

Strangely enough, brands and corporations let them get away with it. In a way it shows just how powerful such emotion carriers are, as the edgiest marketing and communication experts, and the toughest CEOs, fall for them as swiftly as anyone else does. Many times we have seen these experienced business leaders as jaw-dropped as children when meeting an actress or their favourite football player. It is no wonder they forget they are signing them huge cheques for some form of investment return.

A drawback from the relative inexperience of marketers in using emotion-carrying assets is their reluctance to use them with great ambition. Such assets are usually poorly integrated in proper marketing and communication platforms. They are not leveraged across all possible communication tools including advertising, PR, digital, events, social media and so on. Communication and marketing executives feel they are using a powerful tool, but do not sufficiently recognise how important it is to use it properly for their own purposes.

"Many times we have seen these experienced business leaders as jaw-dropped as children when meeting an actress or their favourite football player. It is no wonder they forget they are signing them huge cheques for some form of investment return."

A brand may, for example, be a recognised and legitimate partner of a blockbuster. But if there is no investment to explain why the brand is a partner, no tie-ins, no dedicated promotion, no emotional elaboration, then most of the potential will be lost. The return on investment, which could have been stratospheric, becomes disappointing. Therefore, if we want to understand this integration of an emotional marketing asset within a proper marketing platform better, we need to push the boundaries of traditional media. This is where multi-sense, UGC, emotional sponsorship and other techniques we have seen will come into play.

Measurement and tracking

We discussed earlier in the book how ignorance of actionable information on emotions has led to the sidelining of emotions in the work of marketers. It has also given rise to the belief that the emotional element of marketing campaigns cannot be readily evaluated. The same sorts of straightforward statistical model that judge traditional communications' effectiveness are presumed to be unavailable, so notions of visibility, mediatisation and PR potential are preferred. Emotions are perceived as elusive and volatile, in contrast to hard facts such as media buying, audience profile and media coverage.

But this lack of consideration is absolutely unjustified. It can indeed be difficult to measure a consumer's emotions without invading his privacy or distorting the accuracy of his emotions (asking someone to verbalise his emotion is asking him to translate – thus, inevitably, distort or fail to do full justice to – what he felt). But, as we saw in section 2.3, several measurement techniques can be used to represent, understand and monitor one's emotions.

Marketing and communication: from 'logos' to 'pathos' with 'ethos'

Going back to Ancient Greece enables us to trace a parallel between Rhetoric, the time-honoured art of verbal persuasion, and marketing, the modern art of multimedia persuasion.

The three modes of persuasion used in rhetoric classify the speaker's (or, for us, the brand, product or service's) appeal to the audience. They are divided between *ethos*, *pathos* and *logos*.

Aristotle's 'On Rhetoric' describes these modes of persuasion as:

> "a sort of demonstration, since we are most fully persuaded when we consider a thing to have been demonstrated. Of the modes of persuasion furnished by the spoken word there are three kinds…Persuasion is achieved by the speaker's personal character when the speech is so spoken as to make us think him credible [ethos]…Secondly, persuasion may come through the hearers, when the speech stirs their emotions [pathos]…Thirdly, persuasion is effected through the speech itself when we have proved a truth or an apparent truth by means of the persuasive arguments suitable to the case in question [logos]."

Translated into marketing terms:

- **Ethos** is the brand's authority, credibility and/or honesty, communicated through context and style. It is how good the brand is at convincing the audience that it is the right actor to discuss and offer solutions on a particular topic.

- **Pathos** is tapping into the audience's emotions. In Aristotelian rhetoric this is the use of metaphors, passionate speech, or intimate claims, all of which can be directly adapted in modern marketing. The Andrex puppy (metaphor); the chirpy slogan (passionate speech); the to-camera testimony (intimate claims) are all primitive examples of this. Brand collaboration and UGC, for example, we have seen already as more advanced and effective opportunities for this. Pathos can be particularly powerful if used well. Most communications cannot, however, solely rely on pathos. To be fully effective, the brand has to intimately connect with the target, so pathos should be (as we will argue) matched with ethos.

- **Logos** is a message's logical appeal. Usually, it involves displaying supportive facts and figures. Using the logos and the ethos routes together is interesting, as it positions the brand as a knowledgeable and trustworthy one. However, too much data can be confusing and cold, leading to the conclusion that the brand is dealing with facts and figures rather than human consumers. And, as we have seen, the consumer is not the rational robot who will find largely logos appeals that... appealing.

Traditional advertising is mostly about *logos*. This, of course, has fundamental flaws that we have already gone over earlier in the book. Emotional techniques are more about *pathos*. And the three-fold division of the art of persuasion is a helpful means for drawing out an additional element that must not be overlooked by them. Emotional techniques also require a strong *ethos*.

If the former is not matched with the latter, in sufficiently sophisticated ways, a brand risks falling foul of inauthenticity – and voiding the whole effort. Generating an emotional link with consumers ultimately for marketing purposes will collapse if the consumers believe that the link is purely for marketing purposes.

The unfortunate efforts of corporate social responsibility (CSR)

However, though ethos has taken on greater prominence in the general communications of brands and companies in the past decade, this has not been as effective as it could have been. We need to learn from the mistakes of the past if we are to match effective ethos with effective pathos.

The classic case of Cadbury's "Get Active" campaign is fascinating for this.

E.g.

THE CADBURY CASE – AN ETHOS DEBACLE

In 2003, Cadbury secured the endorsement of top athletes and the sponsorship of the Youth Sport Trust with the Minister of Sport.

The idea behind the agreement was to set up and promote a corporate social responsibility programme aimed at offering sports equipment for children in the UK, based on the consumption of Cadbury's products.

However, the UK's Food Commission quickly calculated that, under the scheme, one set of nets and posts would require the purchase of more than 5,000 chocolate bars.

The 160 million tokens made available by Cadbury equated to a purchase of 2 million kilos of fat, or the consumption of 36 billion calories by British kids...

Even worse, *The Guardian* reported that a 10-year-old child consuming enough bars to get his school a basketball would be required to play the game for 90 hours just to burn off the calories ingested. The Food Commission derided the combination of a fitness campaign with eating chocolate.

Cadbury tried to justify the scheme as healthy but could not fight the bad PR and impressive numbers calculated by the press. Despite being a much-loved brand, the campaign backfired ferociously and had to be cancelled.

Worse still, cumbersome and unsubtle CSR suffers from guilt by association. There have always been examples of malign economic players trying to hide their misbehaviour behind philanthropy, and using it for marketing and communication purposes in a purely cynical fashion.

Particularly poor forms of ethos (however genuine and legitimate) therefore suffer because they are guilty of:

- **lack of relevance to the core business**. If there is no link to be found between a brand and, say, its CSR or explicit ethical commitments, the consumer's assumption is invariably either that it is naked cynicism or irrelevant box ticking.

- the **personal implication of the CEO or the top management** in these initiatives. A personal interest and concern is good, but any kind of financial or other personal gain to be had from it – even if only hypothetical – is to be avoided.

- **how these activities are publicised**. If these ethos initiatives
  are only ever mentioned because they are being explicitly (and
  expensively) broadcast, they are clearly not being effective
  enough – and they will run into the exact eyewall problems
  that more emotionally intelligent communications are meant
  to avoid.

So effective ethos needs to be naturally matched to a brand, have
no obvious connection with furthering a brand's commercial
interests, and be communicated by example rather than
explanation.

A quick and compelling example of this would be the Pepsi's
Refresh Project program, launched in 2010 on social networks,
through which Pepsi pledged to award more than \$20 million in
grants to consumers presenting the best project to improve health,
arts and culture, the environment and education in their
communities. The project worked by asking the global community
to vote for projects that require funding (between \$5,000 and
\$250,000 a month) in local communities.

The ethic of emotional communication

Persuasion is a powerful thing. In modern societies, where
revolutions come at the sharp end of a speech, and mobs rush to
the barricades of Facebook groups and Twitter campaigns, the
greatest currency is opinion. Imposing certain thoughts on the
minds of other people is the focus of some of the most prominent
and important industries out there: journalists, lawyers and of
course brands spend most of their time attempting to do little else.

And if most of us are happy to live with such a continuous
pressure (variously called the marketplace of ideas, the public
square or the information age), it is because we all believe we have
free will. In other words, we all have the ability – real or illusory is
another debate – to accept, modify or reject competing opinions
as we wish.

There is, however, no such thing as free will when it comes to what we feel. You can never choose to feel or not to feel an emotion at a particular point in time. Remember: emotions are reactions – you undergo an emotion because something has provoked it.

For this reason, the use of emotions in communication must be governed by serious ethical standards.

In most countries, advertising already has a set of ethical standards and tends to be tightly regulated and controlled. Advertising professionals have always tried to promote self-regulation but it is, as in many areas, better to have independent third-party regulators far from any conflict of interest to make sure consumers (especially children) are protected from false or dangerous messages.

"Beginning to use emotions in a more systematic and professional way opens up Pandora's box."

Classic regulations in marketing and communication include significant data protection, anti-tobacco and anti-gambling rules, and, strangely enough, sometimes very strict anti-alcohol rules (cf. the 1991 "Evin" law in one of the countries that leads the world in alcohol consumption per capita: France).

Beginning to use emotions in a more systematic and professional way opens up Pandora's box. If marketing and communication professionals become savvy enough to go through the eyewall and make their way into the brain of their target audience against the latter's will, they will have attained a serious power open to serious abuse. It would, potentially, be similar to subliminal advertising – a practice that, whilst of limited proven efficacy, is nonetheless justly banned across most of the world.

The natural and (as we have seen) ruthlessly adaptable cynicism of the human consumer is a reassuring bulwark against such malpractice. Techniques such as brand endorsement and product placement could be said to have developed in the past as means of slipping past the audience's defences, rather like emotional communications today, by reaching beyond the techniques of straightforward communications. But, as we saw in earlier chapters, such approaches were soon seen through – and now only succeed by dint of authenticity. So too, it is to be hoped, will consumers' shrewdness force emotional-marketers to communicate legitimately and authentically or not at all.

As we have seen throughout this book, such legitimacy and authenticity seems already to be an essential component in successful emotional marketing.

> **"Emotional communication can be seen as a highly humanised form of communication. It should demand an extra bit of soul, honesty and ethics from professionals."**

Nevertheless, whilst we trust in the ability of the human mind to defend itself against undue manipulation – and we know it is early days and the dangers are still somewhat theoretical – we recommend the following guidelines for this new way of communicating.

- Show **respect** for the consumer: remember that when you engage the consumer through his emotions, you enter into his most intimate sphere.

- Show **discernment**: while most consumers are experienced enough to deal with traditional persuasion techniques aimed at suggesting what they have to think, there is nothing more intrusive than suggesting to them what they have to feel. Emotions being reactions, there is no equivalent to the freedom of thought in the realm of emotions.

- Show **creativity**: remember than our brains love to be fooled, but only by clever – and harmless – tricks. A consumer will always praise a brand that was clever enough to surprise him, especially in this time of increasing defiance toward brands. But a brand that deceived him will not appear clever but devious.

- Be **dutiful**: if the message cannot be advertised in a traditional fashion, as per advertising regulations, then attempting to communicate it more obliquely through emotional marketing must also be avoided.

By building their communications around emotions, marketing professionals move from telling a story to consumers, to engaging in a conversation with them. Emotional communication can, therefore, be seen as a highly humanised form of communication – it touches the consumer more deeply, and starts a true and sincere dialogue with them. This humanisation of communication should both demand, and inevitably involve, an extra bit of soul, honesty and ethical consideration from professionals.

It is both the 'cost' and essence of the whole medium. It is ultimately the medium's whole advantage.

4.3 The view from the boardroom

Those in the boardroom might be expected to view all this talk of emotional communication with a somewhat jaundiced eye. Affairs of the heart are not, after all, their primary concern, but balance sheets, management methods and growth strategies. The creative side of their business can hardly be expected to be their primary concern.

Nevertheless, though they will not themselves necessarily be in the creative departments of their business, their business is almost certain to have to call upon creativity at some level – whether in advertising to consumers, hiring a PR agency, giving their CEO media training, etc. They will likely have invested in corporate literature. And at the very least they will have a website that has been designed to present the corporation in the most favourable light.

This means that whether a firm sells soaps, IT services or steel, it needs an emotionally informed understanding of how best to present itself to its various stakeholders. Across the board, the right chord has to be hit: the right 'vibes', as it were, need to be communicated to shareholders, to staff, to consumers; and maximum empathy with the company needs to be achieved at every level.

The problem for the boardroom is that this might seem to run counter to their ultimate objective. The primary motivation of top management is to create value for their shareholders. This is a rational objective, and we certainly have no argument with it. But it is a common mistake to address a rational objective with a purely rational mindset. It is easier, for instance, to reorganise a department by showing a new organisation chart which will optimise resources and generate immediate savings of 5%, rather than by justifying the reorganisation on the basis that the new departmental boss will get along better with his or her team. The latter will create a better working environment, and true team efforts to find solutions. This higher efficiency, although qualitative and emotional, will ultimately translate into financials. But it cannot be benchmarked with the 5% immediate savings; and so will probably not be the chosen solution.

The requirement for systematic rational justification in business decisions may encourage sub-optimal choices. The heavier the governance constraints on the business – and this is especially true for large listed corporations having to explain their decisions to analysts on a quarterly basis – the higher the barriers to making emotional (though more efficient) decisions. Family businesses do not have such limits and this is often an advantage for their management. This includes making choices based on gut feeling on strategy, organisation, HR, and of course marketing and communication.

It is likely that the under-representation of women at top management levels makes emotional-based approaches to business more difficult and time-consuming. Women have a better ability to include emotions in their thinking process. It is a long known weakness of many corporations of any size that the lack of females at top management narrows the scope of answers to business issues – especially people-related issues, which are increasingly critical. In 2009, although women represented over half of America's workers, only 12 Fortune 500 companies (or 2.4%) and 25 Fortune 1000 companies (or 2.5%) had women as CEOs or presidents. That same year only 15.7% of board members in Fortune 500 companies were women.

This creates a chicken-and-egg situation: boardrooms are not conscious enough of the necessity to include emotions in their organisation and their business marketing, hence are not motivated to improve the root of the problem by elevating women to board levels.

SUMMARY

Emotional marketing methods

- Celebrities are emotionally powerful elements in marketing, but most marketing campaigns fail to fully capitalise on their use of them. Showing a celebrity alongside your brand is increasingly ineffective: authentically involving him or her in it, in your products and promotion, is the best route today to facilitating emotional identification for the consumer as opposed to cynical revulsion.

- Straightforward sponsorship can be miserably ineffective. Instead, marketers should leverage what sports always convey, and convey similarly everywhere: emotions. Emotions are the richest assets of sponsorship as they are the very reason why people attend to sport events or watch it on TV. Emotions are the reason why consumers are exposed to…sponsored events!

- Product placement works by placing brands in the midst of a highly emotional experience. By doing so, marketers can associate their brands with a situation that inspires, moves or thrills the consumer.

- Experiential marketing that taps into a consumer's social identity, lifestyle and ambitions can be not only emotionally persuasive and memorable, but also one of the most readily viral forms of marketing out there, thanks to the power of mirror neurons.

- User-generated content requires the provision of powerful and accessible platforms. Applied to products as well as promotion, it can be doubly effective at reaching the consumer: in effect making them a brand collaborator, a potent emotional investment.

- The timing of a campaign is more important than ever: the wider emotional context of a community or industry needs to be taken into account.

- Ethical credentials are an important adjunct to effective emotional appeals. They, too, need to be similarly broadcast with subtlety and authenticity. All the innovative emotional marketing in the world, if it depends at the same time on old-fashioned shouting about the ethical qualities of a company, will avail nothing.

 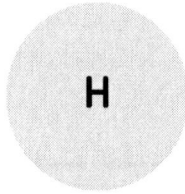 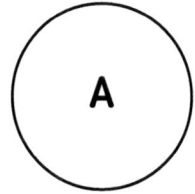

 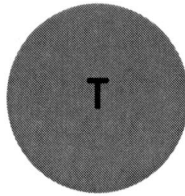 

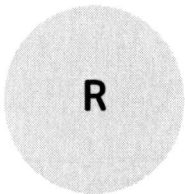 

" The heart has its reasons that reason does not know. **"**

– Pascal

Share of Heart, the New Paradigm of Communication

CHAPTER 5

T he more a brand is visible, the more it will be seen. Axiomatic, at the heart of all marketing, today more than ever, and utterly false.

Being visible is not being seen, no more than seeing is believing. As demonstrated by Simons and Chabris's (1999) 'invisible gorilla' experiment, being visible – even in the middle of a screen – never ensures anything will be seen. When instructed to count how many times a team of three moving players passed a basketball to each other, half of the subjects (Harvard University students) exposed to the experiment did not notice the gorilla who strolled into the middle of the action, faced the camera, thumped its chest, and then left, spending nine seconds on screen in total.

How could something so obvious go completely unnoticed?

What this famous experiment about selective attention teaches us is that you cannot equate exposure to reception. Even an audience seeing your communication, when it is in front of them, is not guaranteed; let alone anything more profound.

135

For this reason alone, companies should be seriously questioning the real benefit of a high share of voice as an objective for their marketing.

Another paradigm is necessary, one that values clever, relevant and effective communications, rather than those that just make the loudest noise. To that end, we suggest seeking consumers' share of heart, rather than focusing on a brand's quest for share of voice.

5.1 Share of voice: less and less audible

BrandChannel describes 'share of voice' as the media spending of a particular brand when compared to others in its category in a given time period.

This advertising weight is still a key decision-making criterion for many brands, especially those which are mass market. Why? The assumption is that the more people hear about you, and the more times they hear your message, the more they buy your product.

This is simplistic. And, we believe, wrong – as much of this book has demonstrated. Rather than reprise those arguments, a straightforward counter-example will show that it can hardly be taken as a rule, and that something else must be going on behind the scenes when it does work.

In the time of the dotcom bubble of the late nineties/early noughties, billions of dollars were invested by brands and products purely into establishing this 'share of voice'. The results were poor. Some of them hardly generated even a few dollars in sales, despite the huge investments, and despite seemingly being businesses that might have worked (had they only been able to get customers). This was the case for Webvan, for example; an online grocery business that went bankrupt in 2001, after having consumed 12 billion dollars in two years.

So the concept of share-of-voice marketing has been tested to destruction. Much of its failure is simply because the unsubtle messages of the mass-market brands, as discussed earlier, are now showered down upon consumers in such great torrents that our brains have become ever more adept at

"The more people who are shouting, the closer the effect is to white noise."

skipping them. Indeed the greater the number, the easier it is to switch off; the more people who are shouting, the closer the effect is to white noise.

The share of voice impresses the retail networks, and the salesmen, who feel reassured by the considerable sums of money and effort invested to support their hard task. But the single consumer cannot possibly be half as impressed even by this, for they will never experience or know the totality of the campaign – and where they get an inkling of it, in repeated sights of a certain promotion, they are liable to be weary more than anything else.

Based on our experience with numerous customers and brands, we believe reliance on share of voice is generally used by default rather than by conviction. The economic crisis of 2007-2009 has made this reliance more and more fragile, not least because it is not supported by rock-solid results. In more difficult times, where all expenses must be scrutinised and boardrooms are increasingly challenged by shareholders, alternative models have to be considered.

We have seen in previous chapters how powerful emotions can be for those seeking to communicate with the modern consumer. The future lies in finding such ways for the message to reach the consumer's heart, rather than staying in front of their eyes – and in finding ways to measure the success of this.

5.2 What is 'share of heart'?

'Share of heart' has been initially defined in the *Journal of Consumer Marketing* as the emotional relationship existing between a consumer and a particular branded product, retailer or service provider.[23]

Initially, this notion of share of heart was developed in response to marketers' tendency to over-intellectualise their products – focusing on promises and attributes – while consumers were mostly concerned by their intangible benefits.

Nowadays, marketers have to develop products and services that speak to the consumer on a personal, emotional level. In a nutshell, a product or service that will win consumers' hearts.

According to Day (1989), share of heart stands on a continuum somewhere between share of mind and share of market. It is influenced by share of mind (you have an emotional connection with a product only if this product is part of your life) and is a critical determinant of market share.

"Share of heart is influenced by share of mind and is a critical determinant of market share."

The fury surrounding the Coca-Cola Company's decision to remove the old beverage formulation, back in 1985, from the market is a perfect illustration of what share of heart is. Despite taste tests favourable to the new formula, the abandonment of the old formula elicited negative emotions so strong that the brand eventually decided to keep it. What this example shows is that you cannot change – even for the better – an iconic product, close to the heart of millions of consumers, without eliciting massive protestations. If you do it at all, it must be with the utmost care, subtlety and consent.

E.g.

THE ISNACK 2.0 CASE

Those who have been to Australia at least once over the past 90 years have inevitably been confronted with the dark brown salty food paste, made from brewer's yeast, named Vegemite (owned by Kraft Foods). Vegemite is to the Australians what Marmite is to the British, i.e. a product nobody else can eat without cringing. And as such, over the years Vegemite has become an iconic product, firmly rooted in Australian households, a true flagship of their popular culture.

In June 2009, Kraft released a new version of Vegemite, combining the original Vegemite with cream cheese, and asked a panel of marketing and communication experts to find a name that appealed to a younger market. The panel sought to capitalise on the hype credentials of Apple's iPod and iPhone. The new name – iSnack 2.0 – was announced on 26 September 2009, during the broadcast of the 2009 AFL Grand Final.

On 30 September 2009, only four days after the announcement, and after massive pressure from consumers, Kraft released plans to abandon the iSnack 2.0 name.

Why? Because you cannot do whatever 'marketing-savvy stuff' you want with a brand benefiting from a massive share of heart amongst consumers. There was no problem with the product itself, but Australians simply could not stand to see their iconic brand tarnished by a name that had nothing to do with the brand's heritage, Australian culture, or themselves.

Within days, opinion columns and social networking sites were flooded with disdain and criticism about the iSnack 2.0 name, forcing Kraft to abandon the moniker.

In October 2009, Kraft opened a new poll on its website offering six possible names and revealed the new name one week later – Vegemite Cheesybite – which had received 36% of the 31,000 votes.

Concretely, measuring share of heart requires measuring the consumer's commitment to a brand, the nature and the strength of the emotional bonds he or she has with a brand. This means discovering the feelings associated with the consumption of a brand as well as the reasons why a particular brand is purchased, and continues to be purchased.

Achieving share of heart is paramount for brands eager to be more firmly entrenched in their product category or to build a stronger defence against competitors' promotional efforts.

"Concretely, measuring share of heart requires measuring the consumer's commitment to a brand, the nature and the strength of the emotional bonds he or she has with a brand."

The source of this share of heart comes from conscious and unconscious elements, including history, personal experience, recommendations from friends and family, and of course all publicity messages of any form.

5.3 Content production and distribution is critical to share of heart

Content marketing is a technique based on the creation and the delivery of valuable content to consumers, to attract them to and engage them in a conversation with the brand, whilst being non-intrusive and non-interruptive (and thereby avoiding being skipped or shunned).

A serious step above old-fashioned ploys such as 'advertorials' (adverts loosely disguised as independent magazine content), content marketing includes the provision of online music, videos and other material from recognised and 'independent' names – all in a more or less explicitly branded surrounding. A novel and straightforward example of this came in September 2009, when a car company paid for one week of *The Spectator* magazine to appear online for all users.

A more classical example would be Grey Goose vodka *Iconoclasts* television series that features original encounters between two well-known personalities from different fields, including film and television, architecture and design, fashion, food, music, science and sports. By doing so, Grey Goose chaperones its customers for an inside meeting with the personalities they admire.

Since content can be found everywhere – off and online, from music to design, from sport to charity – it has to be personally relevant to the consumer to emerge from the clutter. And as we demonstrated earlier in this book, what is relevant to someone comes by definition with an emotional label. *It makes me feel something because this is relevant to me; it is relevant to me because it makes me feel something.*

This what French radio station Radio Nova does with its *"Nova aime…"* label, used to identify and present to listeners any kind of independent content (music, cinema, arts, etc.) that they personally feel strongly about, and think the listener will too.

One of the greatest benefits of content marketing is to make the consumer look forward to receiving a brand's marketing. In this way does it attain a consumer's share of heart.

Content produced by the user

What is a better way to communicate for a brand than a communication designed and relayed by its own customers? What is better than a communication in which each spokesperson or ambassador is actually a user (and a lover) of the brand?

When the consumer starts to contribute to the brand's content himself, this is an entirely new – and promising – form of relationship that is opened up between the brand and the consumer. This gains a share of heart by asking the consumer to creatively engage with its offerings: and, as per 'Emotion and creativity: the motivational power of emotions' (in Chapter 3, page 67), this is a richly and intensifying emotional experience.

A famous example of this is the Converse Gallery co-creative campaign, which in 2006 asked consumers to give their own interpretation of the brand in a TV advertisement. The programme's main restriction – a 23-second time limit – smartly allowed a seven-second space for a sales message in case the spot should ever be aired on TV. The result has been a vast gallery of consumer-generated materials, truly creative, meaningful and emotional.

More recently, Ben & Jerry's 'Do the world a flavour' was an international online competition asking customers to submit a new recipe for their favourite ice-cream brand, with a commitment to produce the winning one.

User-generated content (UGC) has created a lot of buzz, and rightly so, over the last few years. It is an excellent tool to create a two-way communication between a brand, product or corporation and the consumer. The brand, product or corporation plays the role of an enabler (enabling the creation, publishing, or distribution of a message) for the consumer. This is very far removed from the traditional sender-receiver relationship that share of voice would have us pursue. As enabler, instead you provide genuine added value to the consumer's life, and establish the consumer as central, with the brand, product or corporation doing its best to value him or her.

This is, you will notice, at heart what all marketing has ever sought to do – in all forms. *Buy our product, because it's a good product for you.* But with UGC this is not only conveyed but demonstrated, and emotionally sealed.

5.4 The conveyability of the message

Content production and distribution is still going to be necessary with these and other more emotional, creative forms of communication. Although an emotional message is coherently devised, and designed in an effective way, it may not be conveyed properly. It must then be wrapped into a communication medium – whether visual, oral or multi-sensorial – suitably calibrated for the message's content, targets and ambitions. Ultimately the audience will absorb the medium and the message as one (see Chapter 3, the section 'Feeding the message: emotions and brand knowledge' on page 79), so this needs to both veil and articulate the emotion with appropriate subtlety – and clarity.

E.g.

THE PLEASANT SURPRISE OF WAITING

Dutch airline KLM perfectly understood the core of emotional communication and brilliantly implemented it in their Foursquare-based "KLM Surprises" campaign.

The insight was simple: because of waiting times (registration, customs, boarding), traveling is not always that exciting and most passengers have to fight boredom while they wait.

And the challenge even clearer: how could KLM make its passengers feel special while waiting for their flight at Schipol Airport? And turn an emotion – boredom – into another: happiness?

To do so, KLM made a great use of social media. Throughout November 2010, every time a passenger checked-in at a KLM Foursquare location within Schipol Airport, the KLM Surprise Team went on Twitter and Facebook to find out more background and public information about the person. Hence, using the passenger's Twitter and Facebook status, they could find enough content to decide upon a relevant gift and offer it to the passenger in the boarding room.

For consumers craving realness and consideration, these random acts of kindness gave a human face to the brand...and were rewarded as such: in less than two months, KLM registered 1,000,000 impressions on Twitter and more than 45,000 views on YouTube. But more importantly in this age of social media, KLM showed us that creating a real smile on a consumer's face is far more powerful than attaching a smiley face to a communication.

The quality of the emotional conveyer will also determine a message's capacity for going viral (see 3.3, page 87).

In all this a parallel can be draw with medical science: molecules are wrapped into other molecules in order to get into a cell and cure. They cannot get through alone, as they would be blocked by the cell's envelope; or, even going through, they would be destroyed by the cell's safety mechanisms.

SUMMARY

Gaining a share of heart

- Seeing isn't even seeing any more. The marketing objective of the share of voice has been tested to destruction.

- Share of heart stands on a continuum somewhere between share of mind and share of market. It is influenced by share of mind (you have an emotional connection with a product only if this product is part of your life) and is a critical determinant of market share.

- You cannot change – even for the better – an iconic product, close to the heart of millions of consumers, without eliciting massive protestations. If you do it at all, it must be with the utmost care, subtlety and consent.

- Concretely, measuring share of heart requires measuring the consumer's commitment to a brand, the nature and the strength of the emotional bonds he or she has with a brand.

- Content creation (branded free content) and UGC are critical methods for this.

- Emotional messages need to be wrapped into suitably calibrated communication mediums.

 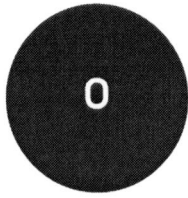 

 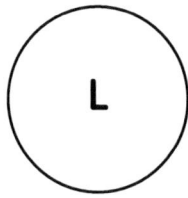 

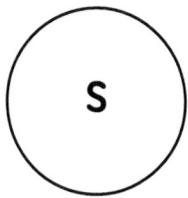 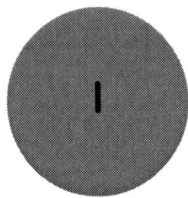 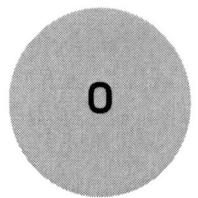

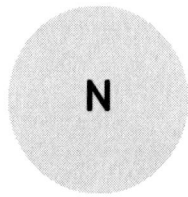

Emotions are Not the Key, They are the Door

No quote for the conclusion?

W hen approaching the end of writing *Emoti-coms*, as authors we argued over a potential quote for the conclusion. One very much liked a saying of Arthur Bloch (the author of Murphy's law): "a conclusion is the place where you get tired of thinking". Only this might, at a first glance, be considered disrespectful of the reader!

On reflection, though, tiredness of thought seemed – if not worthy of the chapter quote – at least very relevant to the case we have made throughout this book for a new, empathic, and ultimately more engaging form of marketing and communication. *Tired* is precisely what most of our brains are when it comes to traditional communications and promotions. After all, whatever goes through the eyeball has to be processed – even superficially – by the brain. And the sheer quantity of data being launched at the modern consumer is manifestly exhausting.

"To target all our advertising at a pre-mapped army of Mr Spocks is, needless to say, an insane method of proceeding."

Emotions, however, are never tiring for our brains to process. Even if they are provoked by a communication stimulus, emotions do not require any intellectual effort from the brain but only *natural* mechanisms that are used similarly in any other situation by the consumer.

Emotions of course resonate within the consumer's brain, triggering some very basic responses (surprise, curiosity, rejection), which will perhaps then become more elaborate later in the process, and conjoined with intellectual effort depending on what, and how important, the situation is for the consumer.

But that is the beauty of emotions for both consumer and marketer. As well as being, as we have seen, powerful and effective – they are also wonderfully economical. If the consumer is not emotionally engaged, they do not expend intellectual effort. So emotional communications should, in the long term, be less stressful and tiring – as well as more invigorating and substantial – for all concerned. Even those emotional communications that miss their target have at least not imposed upon that target very much for the duration of their failure.

What conclusion for our business readers?

We have seen in this book that doing business in general, and more specifically conveying the appropriate message to valorise a brand, is far from being an entirely rational process.

Although most communications campaigns today are supported by research, leveraged by databases, nicely gift-wrapped with creative images and baselines full of impact, the *rationale* behind all of this excellent effort is to target a pre-mapped army of Mr

Spocks. Supremely unemotional, superabundantly rational, and with only slight differences allowed between groups of them in order to justify the nuances in the message or the medium, this is – needless to say – an insane method of proceeding.

Marketing typologies and segmentations only cover one or maybe two facets of consumers: their behaviours and, in some cases, their thought patterns. By doing so, they fail to address the hidden part of the consumer iceberg, what makes them the human beings they are, what really motivates them, what really explains their loyalty and their reactions to communication: their emotions.

Therefore, if these typologies and segmentations can prove useful in selecting the appropriate media-buying strategy, based on what media homogeneous groups of consumer usually consume, they do not suffice in feeding, guiding and implementing the proper message.

What conclusion for the communications industry?

People in charge of business or government communication have to be more conscious of the power of emotions. Marketing and communication executives, professionals working in agencies, media, sports or arts institution are critical to this matter. They are the ones charged with manipulating given messages and making them successes or failures.

If they do not want to have a moral dilemma similar to Einstein's when he realised that his relativity theory was the foundation of the atomic bomb, they have to carefully consider that emotions are consumers' greatest strength and most terrible weakness.

They are our greatest strength since emotions mount perceptual defences based on personal relevance – said differently, what is close to our heart – whilst enabling us to grab the extreme complexity of our world in a snapshot; and our most terrible weakness, since emotions give a direct access to and exert a direct influence on our decision-making process, questioning our free will and allowing us to be influenced with relative ease.

Therefore, managers should be more interested in the emotional impact of their communication than the number of eyeballs they have reached. And, more generally, marketing and communication professionals should have more training in behavioural economics and neurosciences to make sure they do not just replicate old recipes but move forward in the understanding of their target audiences, and how to reach them efficiently.

This book shows emotions as the ultimate communication tool. And as with any tool, emotions can be misused and become dangerous. It is up to the communication professionals' ethics and honesty to use this tool responsibly.

Ethics: the necessity of using emotion as a tool and not as a weapon

Talleyrand made this interesting conclusion about the faculty to talk – and therefore to communicate: "Language was given to humans so that they could disguise their thoughts." In other words, and none of our readers will be learning this for the first time now, providing misleading information, making unreasonable promises or telling false stories are sadly part of marketing and communication.

With emotional communication this is, in many respects, more troubling.

The main difference between cognition and emotion, as far as communication is concerned, is that the consequences of a misleading belief are not as unfortunate as those of a misleading emotion. Why? Because when you are wrong in what you think, it is always possible to find the proper counterarguments that will make you think something closer to reality; it is just a matter of free will. But when it comes to emotions, you cannot be wrong in what you feel. And no matter what someone else tells you about what you feel or what he feels, well…it will still remain between you and yourself. For better and for worse.

This is why professionals must be so cautious when using emotions in communication. Of course, what differentiates emotion-based communication from pure propaganda relies precisely on the communicator's intentions. As discussed earlier, emotion is a great tool for communication. But it is up to professionals – their honesty and ethics – to make sure that they keep using emotions as a tool rather than as a weapon.

At the end of the journey

The results of our search for the links between emotions and communication have proven richer than we expected. We hope you feel the same way about this book, our attempt to distil as much of it as possible into a provocative and above all accessible read. Emotions are thought of as a mysterious, impractical subject; but that need not be the case. A number of disciplines, including neuroscience and psychology, have allowed us to seek and find actionable insights into this vital element of human life.

When we started this search, we were convinced – partly by experience, partly by intuition – that emotions were some kind of key for those having to communicate messages to target audiences. But we found out that emotions are much more important than that.

Instead we have learned how *deeply* the brain relies on emotion over intellect in decision-making, and the overwhelming impact of emotions in our decision-making processes. We have also seen how emotionally induced behaviours or thoughts could actually become almost objects jumping from brain to brain, avoiding the walls of our conscious control.

Emotions are much more important than little keys opening doors; they are the continuum between the outside world and our conscience. Ludwig von Beethoven said that "[m]usic is the mediator between the spiritual and the sensual life". That would be a good description of the role of emotions, too; and marketing communications should adapt to benefit from, or even sometimes be, this space between the spiritual and sensual life.

Emotions are not the key, they are the door.

:-)

 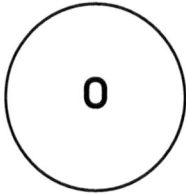 

 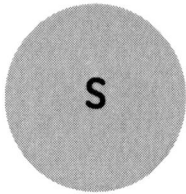

[1] See: www.miqel.com/jazz_music_heart/vibrational-truth.html.

[2] Different studies lead to significantly different results:

> Argyle et al. (1970), 'The communication of inferior and superior attitudes by verbal and non-verbal signals', *British Journal of Social and Clinical Psychology*, 9, 221 -231.

> Hsee et al. (1992), 'Assessments of emotional states of others: Conscious judgments versus emotional contagion', *Journal of Social and Clinical Psychology*, 2, 119-128.

[3] These statistics represent information consumed at home and outside for non-work-related reasons, such as going to the movies, listening to the radio, or talking on a mobile phone. Statistics were computed by aggregating hours of TV, radio, mobile phone, movies, DVD, video games, books and internet consumed at a national level. It does not include information consumed by individuals in the workplace.

[4] According to market research firm IDC (bit.ly/gwkDJt).

[5] Though affect is ordinarily a verb, in psychological studies the term is used in the noun form.

[6] 70% in food retail stores (POPAI Benelux, 2006); 76% in consumer electronics stores (Sony Belgium, 2007); 90% in DIY retail stores (BDA, 2005).

[7] Izard, C. E. (1977), Human Emotions, (Plenum Press: New York).

[8] Dolan, R. J. (2002), 'Emotion, Cognition, and Behavior', *Neuroscience and Psychology*, 298 (5596), 1191-1194.

[9] *Encyclopaedia Britannica*.

[10] See:

> Izard, C. E. (1977)

> Ekman P. (1992), 'Are there basic emotions?', *Psychological Review*, 99, 550-553

> Scherer, K. R. and Wallbott, H. G. (1994), 'Evidence for Universality and Cultural Variation of Differential Emotion Response Patterning', *Journal of Personality and Social Psychology*, 66, 310-328.

[11] Zajonc, R.B. (1980), 'Feeling and Thinking: Preferences Need No Inferences', *American Psychologist*, 35 (2), 151-175.

[12] Named after Hyder, P. and Heath, R. (2005), 'Measuring the Hidden Power of Emotive Advertising', *International Journal of Market Research*, 47 (5), 467-486.

[13] Source: IMS Health report (2009).

[14] Source: www.nytimes.com/2007/02/06/business/media/06adco.html.

[15] Rowe et al. (2007), 'Is the prefrontal cortex necessary for establishing cognitive sets?', *Journal of Neurosciences*, 27, 13303–13310.

[16] Goldberg, M. E. and Gorn, G. J. (1987), 'Happy and Sad TV Programs: How They Affect Reactions to Commercials', *Journal of Consumer Research*, 14 (3), 387-403.

[17] LaBar, K. S. and Cabeza, R. (2006), 'Cognitive Neuroscience of Emotional Memory', *Nature Reviews Neuroscience*, 7 (1), 54-64.

[18] See:

Pham, M. T. (1992), 'Effects of Involvement, Arousal, and Pleasure on the Recognition of Sponsoring Stimuli', *Advances in Consumer Research*, 19 (1), 85-93.

Walliser, B. (1996), 'Le Rôle de l'Intensité des Émotions Éprouvées par le Téléspectateur dans la Mémorisation du Parrainage', *Recherche et Applications en Marketing*, 11 (1), 5-21.

Bal, C. (2010), 'Emotions et persuasion: proposition d'un modèle affectif de persuasion par le parrainage sportif', Thèse pour l'obtention du doctorat en sciences de gestion, Université Paris 1 Panthéon-Sorbonne.

[19] Pavelchak et al. (1988), 'The Super Bowl: An Investigation into the Relationship among Program Context, Emotional Experience, and Ad Recall', *Journal of Consumer Research*, 15 (3), 360-367.

[20] Source: Petty, R.D. and D'Rozario, D. (2009), 'The Use of Dead Celebrities in Advertising and Marketing: Balancing Interests in the Right of Publicity', *Journal of Advertising*, 38 (4), 37-49.

[21] Carroll, A. (2008), 'Brand communications in fashion categories using celebrity endorsement', *Journal of Brand Management*, 17, 146-158.

[22] Source: DRL Limited received an Innovator Award for this campaign at the 2010 Social Commerce Summit in London.

[23] Day, E. (1989), 'Share of heart: what is it and how can it be measured?', *Journal of Consumer Marketing*, 6, 5-12.

Books and articles referenced in *Emoti-coms*

ABN AMRO Economics Department (2006), 'Soccernomics 2006: Soccer and the economy', edition March 2006.

Argyle et al. (1970), 'The communication of inferior and superior attitudes by verbal and non-verbal signals', *British Journal of Social and Clinical Psychology*, 9.

Baas, M., De Dreu, C. K. W. and Nijstad, Bernard A. (2008), 'A meta-analysis of 25 years of mood-creativity research: Hedonic tone, activation, or regulatory focus?', *Psychological Bulletin*, 134 (6).

Bal, C. (2010), 'Emotions et persuasion: proposition d'un modèle affectif de persuasion par le parrainage sportif', Thèse pour l'obtention du doctorat en sciences de gestion, Université Paris 1 Panthéon-Sorbonne.

Bal, C., Quester P. et Boucher S. (2007), Emotions and Sponsorship Marketing, *Admap*, Issue 486, pp.51-52.

Bohn, R. E. and Short, J. E. (2009), 'How Much Information? 2009 Report on American Consumers', Global Information Industry Center, University of California, San Diego.

Carroll, A. (2008), 'Brand communications in fashion categories using celebrity endorsement', *Journal of Brand Management*, 17.

Day, E. (1989), 'Share of heart: what is it and how can it be measured?', *Journal of Consumer Marketing*, 6.

Desmet, P. M. A. (2004), 'From disgust to desire; how products elicit emotions', in *Design and Emotion: the Experience of Everyday Things*, eds. D. C. McDonagh, P. Hekkert, van Erp, J. and Gyi, D. (Taylor & Francis: London).

Dolan, R. J. (2002), 'Emotion, Cognition, and Behavior', *Neuroscience and Psychology*, 298 (5596), 1191-1194.

Ekman P. (1992), 'Are there basic emotions?', *Psychological Review*, 99.

de Gelder, B. and Hadjikhani, N. (2006), 'Non-conscious recognition of emotional body language', *Neuroreport*, Apr 24; 17 (6).

Feldman-Barrett, L. and Salovey, P. (2002), *The Wisdom in Feeling: Psychological processes in emotional intelligence* (Guilford Press: New York).

Goldberg, M. E. and Gorn, G. J. (1987), 'Happy and Sad TV Programs: How They Affect Reactions to Commercials', *Journal of Consumer Research*, 14 (3), 387-403.

Goleman, D. (1997), *Emotional Intelligence*, (Bantam USA: New York).

Hatfield, E., Cacioppo, J. T., and Rapson, R. L. (1993), 'Emotional contagion', *Current Directions in Psychological Science*, 2.

Hsee et al. (1992), 'Assessments of emotional states of others: Conscious judgments versus emotional contagion', *Journal of Social and Clinical Psychology*, 2.

Hyder, P. and Heath, R. (2005), 'Measuring the Hidden Power of Emotive Advertising', *International Journal of Market Research*, 47 (5).

Izard, C. E. (1977), *Human Emotions*, New York: Plenum Press.

LaBar, K. S. and Cabeza, R. (2006), 'Cognitive Neuroscience of Emotional Memory', *Nature Reviews Neuroscience*, 7 (1).

Lawrence, F. (2003), 'How much chocolate do you need to eat to get a free netball from Cadbury?', *The Guardian*, 29 April 2003.

McClure S. M., Li J., Tomlin D., Cypert K.S., Montague L.M. and Read Montague P. (2004), 'Neural Correlates of Behavioral Preference for Culturally Familiar Drinks', *Neuron*, 44.

Mehrabian, A. and Russell, J.A. (1974), *An approach to environmental psychology*, (M.I.T. Press: Cambridge, MA).

North, A. C., Hargreaves, D. J. and McKendrick, J. (1997), 'In-store music affects product choice', *Nature*, 390 (6656).

North, A. C. and Hargreaves, D. J. (1998), 'The effect of music on atmosphere and purchase intentions in a cafeteria', *Journal of Applied Social Psychology*, 28.

North A. C., Hargreaves D. J., and McKendrick J. (1999), 'The influence of in-store music on wine selections', *Journal of Applied Psychology*, 84.

Pavelchak et al. (1988), 'The Super Bowl: An Investigation into the Relationship among Program Context, Emotional Experience, and Ad Recall', *Journal of Consumer Research*, 15 (3).

Petty, R. D. and D'Rozario, D. (2009), 'The Use of Dead Celebrities in Advertising and Marketing: Balancing Interests in the Right of Publicity', *Journal of Advertising*, 38 (4).

Pham, M. T. (1992), 'Effects of Involvement, Arousal, and Pleasure on the Recognition of Sponsoring Stimuli', *Advances in Consumer Research*, 19 (1).

Rowe et al. (2007), 'Is the prefrontal cortex necessary for establishing cognitive sets?', *Journal of Neurosciences*, 27.

Russell, J. A. (2003), 'Core affect and the psychological construction of emotion', *Psychological Review*, 110.

Sanfey, A. G., Rilling, J. K., Aronson, J. A., Nystrom, L. E. and Cohen, J. D. (2002), 'The neural basis of economic decision-making in the ultimatum game', *Science*, 300 (5626)

Scherer, K. R. and Wallbott, H. G. (1994), 'Evidence for Universality and Cultural Variation of Differential Emotion Response Patterning', *Journal of Personality and Social Psychology*, 66.

Shugan, Steven M (2006b), 'Editorial: Errors in the variables, unobserved heterogeneity, and other ways of hiding statistical error', *Marketing Science*, 25 (3).

Sifneos, P. E. (1973), 'The prevalence of alexithymic characteristics in psychosomatic patients', *Psychotherapy and Psychosomatics*, 26, 270-285.

Simon, H. (1957), 'A Behavioral Model of Rational Choice', in *Models of Man, Social and Rational: Mathematical Essays on Rational Human Behavior in a Social Setting* (John Wiley & Sons: Hoboken).

Simons D. J. and Chabris C. F. (1999), 'Gorillas in our midst: sustained inattentional blindness for dynamic events', *Perception* 28 (9).

Tomkins, S. S. (1984), 'Affect theory', in K. R. Scherer and P. Ekman (eds.), *Approaches to emotion*, (Erlbaum: Hillsdale, NJ).

Tynan, C. and McKechnie, S. (2009), 'Hedonic Meaning through Christmas Consumption: A Review and Model', *Journal of Customer Behaviour*, Vol.8 (3).

Vennetier, Perrine (2005), 'Émotion et perception: Attention, émotion en vue', *Science et vie*, Hors série 'L'empire caché de nos émotions: ce que la science nous dévoile', n° 232.

Walliser, B. (1996), 'Le Rôle de l'Intensité des Émotions Éprouvées par le Téléspectateur dans la Mémorisation du Parrainage', *Recherche et Applications en Marketing*, 11 (1).

Zajonc, R.B. (1980), 'Feeling and Thinking: Preferences Need No Inferences', *American Psychologist*, 35 (2), 151-175.

Zak, P. J., Stanton, A. A. and Ahmadi, S. (2007), 'Oxytocin Increases Generosity in Humans', *PLoS ONE*, 2(11): e1128.

Index

in a business environment 4
emotional 54
information overload 6–8, 74–7
interpersonal 46, 49–50
and interpersonal intelligence
52–3
methods 3–4
techniques 9
verbal and non-verbal 3–4
consumer behaviour. *see also*
decision making
emotional drivers 6, 60, 61–5
emotionality vs. rationality 20–21
impulse and involvement 19–21
needs vs. wants 20–1
the rational consumer 13–7
consumer ratings 114–5
consumerism 7
content marketing 140–2
continuous view of emotions 43–4
control, emotional 49
corporate governance 129
corporate hospitality 116–7
corporate social responsibility 123–5
case study 123–4
creativity 68–9, 114
crowd sourcing 67–70. *see also*
user-generated content (UGC)
customer services 61
cynicism 126–7, 131

D

Darwin, Charles 45
decision making 13, 19. *see also*
consumer behaviour
affect theory factors 17
cognitive error 18
emotional drivers 61–5
impulsive acts 19, 61
maximising utility 14–5
optimisation 15
rationality 13, 14–7, 19–21
role of consumer involvement 20
Dictator Game 71

discrete approach of emotions 42, 44
Doritos, *case study* 67–8
Dove, *case study* 36

E

economic rationality 14–5, 16
electromyography 44
Elliott (affective trigger) 65–7
emoticons 4
emotional communication 54
emotional contagion 87–90, 113
mirror neurons 89–90
and sporting events 89
emotional intelligence 49–53, 55–6.
see also alexithymia
interpersonal intelligence 52–3
intrapersonal intelligence 51–2
emotional vacuum 22–3
empathy 23, 50
engagement 91
environmental influence 33, 37
EQ scores 51
ethics 117–130, 132, 150–1
persuasion methods 126–8
role of management 128–130
ethos 122
case study 123–4
evolution 45
experiential marketing 112–4, 131
case study 113
expressive behaviour 32, 36, 44
extroverts 52

F

Facebook 115
facial expression analysis 44
fairness 73, 91
feelings 31, 63–4
in hierarchy of affect theory 33
femininity 46
free will 125–6
fundamental emotions 42